TRiCK Training

Jan Sharp's

TRiCK Training

YOUR HORSE
TO SUCCESS

ECLIPSE
PRESS

Lexington, Kentucky

Library of Congress Control Number: 2003114092

ISBN 1-58150-110-2

Printed in the United States
First Edition: June 2004

Distributed to the trade by
National Book Network
4720-A Boston Way, Lanham, MD 20706
1.800.462.6420

ECLIPSE
PRESS

A Division of
Blood-Horse Publications
Publishers Since 1916

Contents

Introduction

When I was eleven years old, my parents bought me a six-month-old colt named Rickmar Faharin. Because I had a long wait until he was old enough to ride, I spent time playing games with him. I tied him up in baling twine harnesses and imagined that he was pulling a buggy. I posed him in funny positions and took photographs of him. While watching television, I would see Roy Rogers' horse, Trigger, and try to teach his tricks to my colt. In the beginning I just wanted to have a trick horse like Trigger. Over time I discovered what worked and what did not. I spent hundreds of hours with my colt, climbing all over him and doing anything I wanted with him. Though we were a far cry from Roy and Trigger, I did see results. Soon I began to notice that he seemed far more intelligent and more trust-worthy than our other horses. They were just horses, but he was special.

And so by trial and error, I taught myself a method of teaching horses tricks that has worked for me for more than thirty years with hundreds of horses.

I also found that my method of trick training had many more benefits than just teaching a horse to be cute and impressing my friends. Not only did the horses appear to be smarter, but they also were more excited about learning. I found that when using my trick-training method, the horses became more willing partners in future activities. They even watched my body language so closely that they would often start to perform a trick before being asked. Wild horses became calmer; frightened horses became more trusting; and unbroken horses became more submissive, flexible, and responsive. And when the time came to ride, these horses were far more advanced than those that were merely led and lunged.

As I worked with more horses, I would often get phone calls about horses that were due to be sent to auction and likely slaughter. During the calls I would try to learn some background information about the horses. I bought many of them, sometimes right out of the auction killer pens. These were often young, healthy, purebred, registered horses that were being sent to their possible deaths simply because of behavior problems. If they could be retrained, I thought, perhaps, they could find new homes where they could be enjoyed again. I found, over the years, that these horses often made the best trick horses. They were very watchful of my body language, quick to react, and very intelligent. Once they understood that they were instantly and consistently rewarded for the correct behavior or response, they became very willing students. And once they progressed from trying to respond to responding correctly, they moved forward rapidly in their training.

As a result I now enjoy working with horses that others think are untrainable, because I know the difference that my trick-training method can make in a horse's attitude and behavior. Many of the retrained horses have been given a new lease on life and resold to good homes.

I kept one of the "problem" horses, my stallion TS Black Tie Affair, who appears in most of the photos in the book. His previous owner sold him because the stallion would stand on his hind legs and charge her. After I brought Black Tie Affair home, he charged at me from his stall and bit me twice in the center of my back when I was turned away from him. I immediately taught him some basic skills and how to lie down. The second day I had him, he again charged at me, but when I yelled at him he retreated to the back of his stall where he promptly lay down. He wasn't sure what I wanted but knew that lying down made me happy so that's what he did. It was the last time he ever charged at me. I have owned

TS Black Tie Affair

and shown this stallion in countless shows and demonstrations for ten years now. He is one of ten half-Arabian, black-and-white Pinto horses that I own, and all are both show and trick horses.

I have been invited to perform with my horses at many places. And everywhere I perform, people want to know how they can teach their own horses tricks. Many of these people would be satisfied to teach their horse just one trick since they probably think training their horse must be very difficult. And since most professional trick trainers don't share their knowledge with others, there are few places for anyone to learn trick-horse training.

So the purpose of this book is to help horse owners who not only want to teach their horse tricks, but also want to focus on the many benefits trick training can bring to both horse and owner. For example, a dressage rider might want to teach her horse tricks for the suppleness and submission he develop. A trail rider can use these methods to gain more control and confidence in his horse. A show rider can use the training to improve her horse's head set and carriage in the show ring. A non-riding owner can gain another way to interact with his horse. Whether your goal is championship ribbons, a safer trail horse, or the simple joy of working with your own horse, my proven method of trick training can help you achieve these goals. And while it's fun to own a trick horse, the real reward comes from developing a more obedient, intelligent, and responsive companion.

(**Note**: For clearer illustrative purposes the horses and handler used to illustrate this book are not wearing protective equipment. For actual training sessions, handlers should always wear an ASTM-approved riding helmet and leather gloves, and equip their horse with leg wraps.)

1

Selecting the Trick Horse

There are few things you can do with your horse that require less money or performance space than trick training. Imagine how much fun it would be to ride to center ring to receive your show ribbon and have your horse take a bow. For the older rider with arthritis, having a horse that can bow down for mounting could make the difference between being able to trail ride without assistance or not. For those owners interested in public exhibitions, nothing could be more thrilling than performing before large crowds.

But remember, a horse is not a toy poodle that performs tricks to be cute. A horse is a thousand-pound prey animal that can panic when a rope gets wrapped around his leg. He can be a strong-willed son-of-a-gun that holds up a group trail ride when he refuses to set hoof on a wooden bridge. Or, he can be an animal that is so spoiled he is a danger to himself and everyone around him.

My trick-training method addresses these problems and can improve your horse in many ways. Who wouldn't want a horse that steps forward when asked, stops, waits, and listens for his next instructions?

Through this training you can ensure that the desired behaviors are carried out in everything you will ever do with your horse — in the barn, on the trail, or in the show ring.

Trick training is done in slow steps. When one movement is mastered, you build on that training and advance to the next step. But trick training also takes time, patience, and hard work from both you and your horse. The first horse you train will also be your most difficult. Until you master the skills necessary to train him, you will make mistakes, so your first horse will also be your practice horse. Your second horse will be easier, and your third even more so. You will learn what works, and what does not, with each horse. Some horses are more responsive to cues. Some are right-handed, and working to the left is harder for them.

One of the benefits of trick training is that you will become more skilled at reading horses' body language and at picking up the slightest flick of an ear and tensing of a muscle. You will be able to tell volumes about a horse just by knowing and watching his eyes. You can usually tell the moment a horse understands something by an immediate softening of his eyes. If you don't yet own a horse, or have several to choose from, here are some tips to help you select the perfect trick-training student to practice on, especially if you eventually want to give public performances with your horse.

Choosing which breed depends on your personal preferences and skill level. There are trick horses in most breeds. Arabians and Arabian crosses are well suited for trick training because they are highly intelligent, beautiful, and sensitive to subtle cues. This sensitivity sometimes makes them too much horse for the timid or beginning handler. Breeds such as the Quarter Horse, Paint, and Morgan have excellent reputations as being very trainable and easy to work around. The colorful markings of breeds such as the Appaloosa make them stand out. If you do not intend to perform with your horse under saddle, then a small pony such as the Shetland or Welsh makes a wonderful trick student. Ponies and miniature horses are very intelligent and clever. They are easier for a beginner to work with and easier to transport to performances in small places like schools and nursing homes. Their size is less intimidating when they are entertaining small children, and they are easier for people in wheelchairs to pet. The draft breeds can be slower and less responsive to the trainer, but a massive trick-performing horse is a sight to behold. Needless to say, a draft horse would need much more performance space than a miniature horse would. All breeds can be trick trained with time and patience.

Look for the horse that is calm and user-friendly. A nervous horse might be spooky working in strange areas or in front of noisy crowds. He cannot concentrate on you if he's worried about scary sounds and smells. Although these types of horses can become exceptional trick horses, they require extra time and effort. To a beginner, this type can be discouraging.

Avoid the dead-broke, sleepy types. These horses have often learned to tune out people and their cues. Kids' horses often fall into this category, especially those that have had a life of rough handling of bit, whip, and spur. This type of horse can be a slow and dull performer and often would rather be left alone. Although trainable, these horses often can be more difficult to train than the hyper, nervous kind.

Pretty is as pretty does. All else being equal, a pretty horse is always desirable. The more unusual the markings or color, the more your audience will remember your horse. A golden palomino, a loud Appaloosa, or a flashy pinto will stand out over the standard bay with no white markings. If your current horse is rather plain, you can glitz him up by wearing a bright costume and using matching leg wraps on him when you perform in public.

The horse should be the right size to fit you. A large rider on a too small horse will make the audience feel sorry for the horse. A small rider on a huge horse also will look just as out of balance, and cueing him may be more difficult. The exception would be ponies and miniature horses that always look cute when exhibited in hand by either children or adults.

Geldings or mares are generally easier to work with. A stallion is just as intelligent and sometimes even smarter and quicker to learn, but he can be more difficult, or even dangerous, for a beginner to work with. In the hands of experienced trainers, many of the top performing horses are stallions, but a stallion can be especially difficult when performing in public. If a nearby mare is in heat or the stallion gets away, you could be in for some embarrassing moments or put yourself and others in danger. I often do demonstrations in show rings that other horses have been in. My stallion will sniff the ground when he is bowing or lying down. You must always be aware he is a stallion and that you may not have his full attention at all times. If you have a difficult stallion, trick training can do wonders for him; that said, however, stallions are best left to experienced trainers and experts.

You Can Teach Any Horse Tricks

Contrary to what you might think, sometimes the less training a horse has before starting, the better. A late yearling can easily master 10 tricks and be looking for more. Trick training is a wonderful way to spend time with a horse too young to be ridden. He will learn how to be patient, how to give to pressure, and how to please his master. When the time comes to start his under-saddle work, he will be a joy to train compared to the horse that has had only the normal halter training or has been left in the pasture to fend for himself. Too many owners basically ignore a colt until he is old enough to be ridden. Before under-saddle training, very little is expected of him. At best, if he is only trained to lead, tie, stand to be groomed, and to allow his feet to be picked up, his owners consider well-trained. A foal can learn to accept an amazing number of things. The more you can do with a young horse, the easier any future training will be for him. A very young colt is easy to push gently into position. The colt learns early that you can control him, and he learns not to resist training. Of course, his lessons need to be modified somewhat from those of an adult horse. Because he has a short attention span, his lessons will need to be kept short, and his training should be modified for his age. At a very young age he can step up onto boxes, walk over ground poles, be taught how to bow, lie down, and even sit. Young horses are usually more willing to pick things up in their mouths than are older horses. Once you establish the habit and reward them for it, they will remember the training as they get older.

A gentle, mature horse is a good selection for beginner trick trainers since he probably has already had a great deal of training in basic ground manners and under-saddle work. He's been around the block and is usually more accepting of new situations and props than an inexperienced horse.

An aged horse will be more set in his ways, and his joints and muscles may be stiff, making some of the tricks more difficult or impossible for him.

No matter the breed or age of your horse, or level of his

current training, you can still enjoy teaching him tricks and reap the many benefits.

The Equine Good Citizen

A well-trained horse is a joy to own. He has respect for his handler and rider. He's relaxed and happy in most situations. He allows himself to be touched on all parts of his body and to be groomed and tacked without fuss. When asked, he stands quietly on a slack lead or rein. He moves off easily when asked and stays at the same speed and direction until asked to change. He's alert to his surroundings but doesn't overly react to them. He's fun to be around and gets along with everyone, animal and people alike. Horses with this disposition are the easiest type to start with. They are already easy to work around, and you can begin their trick training right away. Introducing them to props and obstacles is easy, as they have a natural urge to see things up close and touch them with their noses. They naturally want to pick up and play with things around the barn. Horses that just have to see what you are doing and are usually between you and what you're working on are excellent trick-training candidates.

The opposite is the type of horse that invades your personal space by either rubbing on you or making you duck and dive out of his way. He pulls his lead or reins out of your hands. He snatches mouthfuls of grass whenever he can. He threatens people by turning tail or running them over. He's goosey or resentful when he is being groomed or tacked. He's constantly looking for ways to evade his rider's cues by tossing his head, jigging, or refusing obstacles. Trick training can greatly benefit this type of horse. However, you will first need to spend more time teaching him basic ground manners. You will need to establish yourself as leader with the dominant ones and desensitize the flighty and goosey ones before you can start trick-training work. This bad-actor type will take more time and effort, but the results can be quite rewarding. If possible, use gentle horses as your first few students and save the difficult ones for when you are more experienced.

Leader of the Herd

If you already own a horse and think you know him pretty well, give him this test to see what type of horse you have — an "equine good citizen" or a "bad actor."

Go into his stall and talk to him for a minute.

1) If he approaches you with ears up and a "happy to see you" expression, praise him and give him a pat. Stand in front of him and quickly raise your hand as if you might strike him. He should jerk his head up slightly in surprise, which is natural. Talk to him and give him a pat. Raise your arm up and down slowly until he no longer jerks away and praise him.

Stroke his forehead until he relaxes, drops his head, and softens his eyes. This type of horse is ideal. He is responsive, yet he can relax enough to learn. A horse can only learn when he is relaxed. If he fears for his life, because of real or imagined harm, he cannot learn.

2) If he runs you over or turns his tail to you and threatens you with a possible kick, you have a horse that needs correction before you can proceed. This type either lacks respect or fears you. Contrary to what you might think, the treat-

ment for lack of respect or fear is the same.

Often we think that treats and pats will make a horse love us. We are sometimes rewarded for our good intentions with a horse that kicks, bites, crowds us in the stall, or walks all over us. Why would he be so mean when all we want to do is love him? Horses are herd animals. There is usually one leader and everyone else follows. Most horses are happy to follow if they have a strong leader. You need to be that leader and impress your horse with that knowledge in no uncertain terms. The leader in a herd of horses is the horse that doesn't have bite marks on him. He moves from hay pile to hay pile and the other horses get out of his way. The second horse down in the pecking order makes the third one down move out of his way and so on.

You need to know where you stand in your horse's herd. If you are the one that moves out of his way, then you know that he thinks you are beneath him. You must stand your ground and make *him* move. You do not want to be abusive, but you must gain his respect as well as his trust. There are times when the herd leader will have to use his teeth and hooves to make an impression on his disobedient pasture mates. After that, he rules by flattened ears, bared teeth, and raised hoof. You will earn respect by using your body language, voice, touch, and the cue whip. The cue whip (see Chapter 2) is just an extension of your arm and is not used for punishment or intimidation.

A word of warning: Invading your personal space, taking food from you, and showing aggression are ways a dominant horse displays his dominance over lower-ranked herd members. When you allow your horse to rub on you, search your pockets for treats, or make you move out of his way, you are showing him that he is dominant over you.

2

The First Steps in Learning

As you and your horse work together, you will learn each other's subtle movements and what they mean. It will take time, but to see the bond develop and to build on it is a thrill. There will be days when you think the training is not going to work and you may want to give up. Your horse may put up a real fuss until he starts to understand the cues and connect them with the behaviors you are struggling to teach him. However, the day will come when you will see the "light bulb" go on above your horse's head — when he finally understands what you are trying to do and it starts to make sense to him.

Some types of trick training result in a horse that can only do tricks. My method is different in that you are teaching your horse to be submissive to pressure. You will use this method in every aspect of his life. You cannot force your horse to perform if he is unwilling. You must teach him through firm but gentle training to want to perform for you. He must want to follow your lead and want to please you. A horse that is beaten into performing will harbor a resentment of his trainer that will drive a wedge into the bond that is so necessary to the horse-and-trainer relationship.

Before you can start to think about actual trick training,

your horse must learn the word "whoa" and respect it. When you tell him whoa, his feet must remain motionless and his attention should be directed toward you until you tell him differently. For a well-trained horse, this will be easy as he learned how to stand still in his early basic training and his owners have made sure he has remained respectful. However, with the young or disobedient horse, it will take some practice before he learns to plant his feet and stand motionless in spite of his surroundings. Set up a situation where he is less likely to fail. Start by training him in an area that he is very comfortable in, say just outside his stall, and gradually move him to more stressful areas. With the lead shank chain over his nose, turn and face him and ask him to "whoa" by stopping him with a little tug on his lead. Don't try to hold him in place or feed him treats to make him stand still. You want to show him what you want and then allow him to make the decision to move or not. If he makes the wrong choice, you will correct him. If he makes the right choice, you will praise him. Don't stand directly in front of him but keep facing him. If he moves his feet after you stop him, repeat the "whoa" command and give him one sharp jerk on the shank, enough to cause him to "bug out his eyes" just a little and to tense his muscles. Immediately, let the lead rope slacken. Take a moment to loosen the chain over his nose, pat his neck, and speak kindly to him. If he moves again, repeat the correction. Again show him that while you still like him, you don't like him moving his feet after you tell him whoa. If he stops and stands briefly, then inches forward, back him up to where you originally asked him to stand and repeat your correction. You, and not he, will select where he stops and stands.

Once he will stand quietly, repeat the training in other

areas. First, master the request at home where it's quiet and then gradually add more distractions. Ask him to stand motionless for longer periods in more distracting circumstances. Once he is standing quietly for several minutes, ask him

REMEMBER THIS TIP

Teaching your horse to respect the word "whoa" by insisting that he stand motionless each time you ask him will serve both you and your horse in many ways. Whoa means that the horse's feet do not move.

to stand for a little longer. Correct him for moving his feet, rubbing on you, swiveling his head and neck around, or using his voice.

You must gain your horse's respect and attention before you can start trick training. You cannot train a horse that is constantly moving his feet, pushing you around, or wanting to return to his stablemates. You must be aware of what your body is doing at all times. Work around him in a calm and relaxed manner with your shoulders dropped. Keep your voice soft and reassuring while you are trying to get him to attempt new things, such as stepping up onto a box or lying down. When you need to correct him, drop your voice down and give him a sharp "No." Your horse watches your body language and can see your entire body. You must be consistent in how you carry yourself around him and how you give his cues. He will notice the little things that you are not aware that you do. You may make quick movements that scare him. Your bold stance and direct look may intimidate a timid horse or challenge a bolder, spoiled horse. For every action there is a reaction — even if you don't notice it right away.

Many a horse and/or rider has been saved from grave injury only because the horse remembered his training and stood motionless when asked. No matter what else your horse learns, if he can learn to stop and stand still when asked, he has learned something worth knowing. It is your job to train him to do so correctly. The feet must stop moving. Do not allow him to fuss around, rub on you, and continually shift his feet when he's supposed to be standing still. You cannot make him stand like a statue during one training session and then allow him to fuss around during another. He must stand still each and every time asked. There is no "halfway" or "almost" standing still when asking for the whoa. Whoa means standing motionless each and every time. Period.

Just as important as standing still is teaching your horse not to pull against you. This means when you are leading him, he is not to drag you around by his lead rope or constantly pull away from you to get his head down to grab mouthfuls of grass. Under saddle, he must not shove out his nose to pull the reins from your hands. Every time he pulls against you, you must correct him by a quick, sharp tug on his lead until he no longer tries. When he is under saddle, you can break him of this habit by giving him a quick jab with your heel. As soon as he gives to you, you give back to him with a loose lead. Strive to teach him to stand, walk, or ride with a slack lead rope or rein. Remember that pulling you around and evading your aids are ways your horse shows his dominance over you.

Remember that trick training is supposed to be fun for both you and your horse. If you train with kindness and patience, your horse will look forward to his training sessions. He will enjoy his work and be a willing and happy performer.

If I leave any of my props out where my horses can get them, I find them playing with them. When I let the horses

Tools of the Trade

The tools you will need are very simple and inexpensive. You may already have most of them in your barn.

For your personal protection, you will need the following:
- An approved ASTM (American Society for Testing and Materials) equestrian safety helmet.
- Good leather footwear for traction and protection from your horse's heavy feet.
- Well-fitting leather gloves for better grip and protection from possible rope burns.

For your horse's protection, he will need the following:
- Leg wraps.
- A well-fitted, strong halter.
- A well-bedded, soft, safe, quiet area to work in.

Additional items and equipment:
- A 15-foot, soft, non-stretch rope. A half-inch round, braided nylon or cotton rope works best. Rope length will vary depending on the size of your horse.
- A stiff 48-inch dressage cue whip.
- A stiff buggy whip about five to six feet long with no string attachment.
- A soft, non-stretch lead rope with a chain and snap at one end.
- Treats your horse likes. Apple or carrot slices work well.
- Time and patience.

Things that you do not need:
- A quick temper.
- A lack of patience.
- An inflated ego.

loose in the arena, they race to see what has been left out. They kick the balls, stand on the boxes, pick up the cue whip and carry it around. I once got a call from a neighbor who said something was wrong with one of my horses in the pasture. I ran out to find the horse performing the Spanish Walk (see Chapter 7). It appeared that he was either showing off to the other horses or trying to teach it to them. No wonder my neighbors thought the horse had gone nuts.

Before you start each training session, be sure that your horse has had enough turnout time and exercise to burn off all of his excess energy. Remove all loose dogs, running children, and well-meaning spectators. Tell them that you will give them all a free show when your horse has mastered a few tricks, but not until. You don't need differing advice from the sidelines. You can train your horse by yourself, and you want to be developing a close bond with your horse so you two can be working partners. A one-on-one working relationship will speed the training process and give you a satisfying sense of pride.

However, there are exceptions to training a horse one on one. Young adults, under the age of 18, or beginners may need the help of a responsible adult who has experience working with horses. Because horses are powerful animals and the trainer will be working with ropes and cue whips, young adults or adult beginners should select one person to help whenever needed; otherwise, the horse could become confused by having a different trainer with slightly different cues each day. The experienced adult can either directly help or just quietly sit on the sidelines to lend assistance only if necessary.

A word about "clickers." A clicker is a small, hand-held device that makes a loud clicking sound when you squeeze it. The horse learns to associate a correct response with the clicking sound, which is followed by a food reward. Predator animals such as dogs are especially quick to respond to clicker training.

When I began my trick training work in 1969, no one had ever heard of a clicker. You read a lot about clickers and target training now. Since I am always open to new ideas, I tried the clicker but found it very unhandy. I found I needed more hands than I had. I would have a lead rope in one hand, a cue whip in the other, and the moment the horse responded correctly, I was supposed to click the clicker and give a food reward. It never failed that I had the clicker backward and couldn't click at the exact moment that I needed to. A horse has ears and can hear the spoken word "good" just as easily as he can hear a click. I can say "good" more quickly than I can click a clicker. So, I dispensed with the clicker and used only my voice and hands. I always have my voice and hands with me, and I can put inflection in my voice that the clicker doesn't have. However, many people do successfully employ clicker training.

The Lead Rope and Cue Whip

My horses soon learn that when I take them out of their stall, put on their halter, and put the lead rope chain over their nose, they'd better start paying attention. We might be just taking a walk out to the pasture or we might be headed to a trick-training session. However, as soon as I pick up either of my cue whips, I have their full attention. This attention does not come from fear. They have learned through repetition that my actions of putting the chain over their nose and holding the cue whip mean it's training time. They know what to expect and usually are looking forward to it if I have done their early training correctly.

As you work with your horse, you will fine-tune your whip cues to specific places on your horse's body. Each one will mean a different thing to him. It is your job always to use the same cue at the same place for the same response. Your cue whip is just an extension of your arm and allows you to reach all his cue spots safely. The cue whip is not used for punishment, except in extreme cases. If you have never carried a whip around your horse, or if he has been abused with one in his past, take time to show him it will not hurt him. Gently rub it around on his body and legs until he calmly accepts it. Don't wave your whip around and give your cues in a weak and undirected fashion or you will confuse your horse. Many whip cues are given by just a tap. The cue to bow is a light tap behind the right knee. The cue to lie down is a light tap behind the left knee. To circus bow, the cue is a light tap between his front legs at his girth area. For the Spanish Walk, the cue is a light tap at his forearm. To rear, the cue is lifting the whip above your head and so on. Be specific with your cues.

> **REMEMBER THIS TIP**
>
> Put the chain over your horse's nose and carry your cue whip only when you are actually training or working with him on his tricks. He needs to associate the two actions with attention, respect, and learning.

There might be times when a correction should be made with the whip, such as if the horse attempts to bite or kick you. In that case one fast pop and a harsh word at him will be enough. Correction must be instantaneous and fair. Remember the three-second rule: You must correct him within three seconds or he won't associate the correction with the offense. If you have to leave your horse to go find your whip to correct him, it's too late. After the correction

TRAINING KEY

Since I also train and show Arabian halter horses, I've taught them to know the difference between halter-training time and trick-training time since all my halter show horses are also trick horses. I put the chain over the nose for trick training and under the chin for halter. The horses quickly learn the difference. They lift their heads and strike a halter pose as soon as the chain goes under their chin. I never use the chain under the chin for anything else other than halter training or showing. I place the chain under the chin moments before entering the show ring.

take a few minutes to pet him and rub the whip around his body so he does not fear it.

I'm Sorry

There are two words that all horses seem to understand: "I'm sorry."

Should you accidentally hurt your horse, such as poking him in the eye, stop and tell him that you are sorry. Take a moment to rub his forehead, rub the spot you hurt, and talk to him. If you poked your horse in the eye on purpose, he would learn to fear you and become head shy. However, if you accidentally hurt him and take a moment to tell him that you didn't mean it, he will immediately drop his head and forgive you. You must admit your mistake quickly to him and spend enough time telling him that you are sorry and rub the injury long enough to cause him to relax. It's your job to make him understand that it was an accident.

Treats

The old saying "if it eats, it can be trained" is true. In the beginning I use small treats to reward a horse for any positive effort. As he progresses, I use fewer and fewer treat rewards. Many animals are trained with the old "tease and reward" method. If you have ever seen a dog that will sit up for a treat but will not if a treat isn't dangled over his nose, then you have seen the drawbacks of this method. I don't want to be laden with pockets full of treats for each performance. It would also be very distracting to your audience if you had to wave a treat in front of your horse before each trick then stop and wait while he chewed it. It is also very annoying to be mobbed by your horse constantly looking for his treat. The test of a good trick horse routine is how smoothly it flows from one trick to the next.

A horse does seem to learn faster if he is rewarded with a treat or generous praise and pats for trying. There are exceptions, as in learning how to stand still. You don't reward him for "almost" standing still. He simply has to stand still or be immediately corrected. In that case his reward for standing still is that you won't need to correct him. His reward is the reward of rest and comfort — if he stands still when asked. At the beginning of his trick training, he won't be perfect but still should be rewarded for the attempt. As he advances, he should only be rewarded for a perfect response. As his training continues to advance, he will be working more for your praise, and treats are no longer needed. However, a treat is always welcome at the end of his performance.

Use a small piece of food for his reward. Give it to him and let him finish it. You will not have his complete attention while he is chewing. Don't ask him to do anything more until the treat is finished. You do not want to wait five minutes while he chews a whole carrot. Too many treats can also make him sick. One carrot or apple sliced into many small pieces will work well. Now is not the time to introduce new, unusual, or sticky foods. A pocket or fanny pack filled with sliced carrots and apples or with some oats will be in easy reach and cost nearly nothing. No need for expensive store-bought treats. You need to have the treats with you so you can reward him immediately.

The exception of giving food rewards is when you are working with very young colts. Many of them do not like treats or will not even attempt to try one. In their case you can reward them with a good scratching along their top line while telling them how good they are. Dig your fingers into the base of the colt's mane, the middle of his back, the root of his tail and find all those other itchy places that he can't reach and spend a few minutes satisfying that itch. This is also a very good way to teach a colt to allow all places of his body to be touched. When I have a colt standing up on a box, I can easily reach up under his belly to scratch it for him. At first he may be alarmed but he quickly learns to look forward to it as another form of reward.

We all know that feeding a horse by hand can lead to nipping. If he is given a food treat for each attempt, he will quickly learn to do the trick and reach for your hand for the reward. He will expect it and can become demanding and grabby. If he starts to nip or get pushy, stop the treats. Learning how and when to give food rewards is essential. Never reward him for snatching at your hand for food by giving him the food. Make him mind his manners, repeat the trick, and then give him his treat only when he waits for his reward.

If your horse will not eat a treat he likes during one of your training sessions, stop and figure out why. If he will not eat, he's usually fearful. Stop and review your training methods.

You could be scaring him with your body language or your

> **☞ REMEMBER THIS TIP**
>
> Never reward for bad manners. Never give a treat to a horse that is grabbing or snatching at you for his expected reward.

harsh voice, or you might be going too quickly with his training. Take him for a short, relaxing walk. Rub his muzzle and chin until you feel it go loose and relaxed.

When I get on a horse's back for the first time, I lean over and try to feed him a handful of grain or an apple slice. If he won't eat it, I get off and spend more time with him before getting on again. Tightly clamped lips are a dead giveaway that a horse is tense. In the beginning trick horse, it means he's too tense to learn, and in a beginning riding horse, it means he could be on the edge of a blowup. In either case stop and do some additional basic groundwork before proceeding.

Praise

As a trainer you will learn to use different degrees of praise. You can use your voice to show your horse how happy you are with his behavior. As your horse learns a new trick, you can reward him with a simple, solidly spoken "good" and follow it with a quick, soft stroke to his forehead or neck. However, the moment you see that he fully understands for the first time what you are asking and he performs as desired, heap on the praise. Tell him how wonderful he is, clap, smile, give him several minutes of good patting and rubbing, and reward him with a food treat. Take him for a short, relaxing walk around in a few small circles. You want him to look forward to pleasing you.

It's your job to teach him to want to learn and perform correctly, so save your "prolonged, excited praise" for only those times when he first really understands or performs very well. Give him reassuring praise as he is learning, but go nuts when he understands. If you give him the full "go nuts" treatment every time he makes a move, he will soon learn to tune you out. He will not be able to tell the difference between just any old movement and the movement done correctly. Don't lie to him and tell him that he's wonderful when he was just okay. He will learn to believe you if you tell him he's wonderful only after the times when he really is wonderful. He will learn to seek perfection because sloppy performances will not get him the attention, praise, and rewards that he looks forward to so much.

3

Giving to Pressure

Acceptance of pressure is part of every horse's basic education, whether for trick training or riding. Rather than fight it, your horse will learn to relax and soften his muscles. You will greatly improve communication between yourself and your horse, both in hand and under saddle. Horses that fight pressure become halter pullers when tied and crowd you into their stall walls. When ridden, they ignore your leg cues and resist the bit by tossing their heads. In general they ignore or resist their handler's cues.

While young or disobedient horses will have to learn giving to pressure from the beginning, many mature riding horses can have their prior training enhanced or refined. Even some horses with impressive show records have never learned the finer points of submission and flexibility. They travel around the ring in a stiff frame, while the rider struggles to make it all look good to the judge's eye. Before you begin trick training even a quiet and obedient horse, be sure to test his submission and training by first asking him to give to, and step away from, pressure. If he responds correctly, wonderful, you already own a horse that understands this concept. If not, you will need to teach it to him. All horses must know how to give to pressure before they can move on to learning how to perform tricks. Nearly all tricks require some form of submission.

A horse that gives to pressure is a joy to own and ride. He gives to the bit and to the rider's aids and works in a more relaxed and happy frame. He can be easily led or ridden without resistance. While these things greatly improve your enjoyment of the trail horse, they are absolutely required in the show ring. Show horses are marked down for pinned ears, stiffness, tossed heads, open mouths, and wringing tails — all signs of resistance and lack of submission. Submission does not mean that the horse is so intimidated that he cowers

For less control wrap the lead rope chain once around the halter nose band.

For more control place the lead rope chain over the nose.

before his master. Submission means that the horse is attentive, confident, light, giving, and responsive to his rider's aids.

While it is usually easier to trick train a horse that is gentle and can already be handled easily, extensive prior training is not necessary. In working with many unhandled or spoiled horses, I've found that trick training can work wonders on a horse's mind, whereas some traditional, under-saddle training methods have frightened or unnerved the horse. Too many young horses are basically ignored until they are old enough to be saddle trained. Then they are forced to learn many new things all at once, such as how to balance the weight of a rider and understand and accept all his aids, all without any prior experience or training in how to first give to pressure.

The idea that a horse must be shown who is boss or he'll take advantage of you is the reason many horses have been trained with force alone. Most horses are happy to follow if they have a leader they respect. However, respect is not fear. Fear or resentment will make for unhappy trick horses. You don't need to be harsh or cruel as either can make your horse mad at or afraid of you. At the same time you don't want to go to the opposite extreme. Many well-loved horses have been allowed to become pushy and disrespectful of their owners. You must show your horse what is expected of him, what makes you happy, and what displeases you. You must be consistent, patient, fair, and firm to earn his respect and attention. Once you have that, he's ready to learn.

If you happen to own or have purchased a "man-eater" or a "Pampered Polly" who looks down her royal nose at you, you will need to establish your position as leader before you can move ahead to trick training. With these types of horses, one scenario you may encounter daily is your horse greeting you in his stall by swinging his tail to you in a threatening manner, as if he's preparing to kick — a tail turner.

Maybe he's just bluffing or maybe he really will kick, but it means the same thing to him — "I don't want you to catch me. Leave me alone." Either you chase him around and around in his stall or you go get the grain bucket to catch him. Either way the horse is the leader and you're the follower, doing what it takes to catch him on *his* terms. Some horses derive great fun from making you duck, dive, and run around after them. It's not much fun for you, and it puts you in a dangerous position, directly behind some awfully powerful artillery — the hind legs.

The reason you want to correct a tail turner is so he can be safely approached and caught more easily. It also will help establish your position in his herd as leader, which is necessary if you want to teach him tricks, or anything else, effectively.

Correcting the Tail Turner

What you will need: Leg wraps for all four legs, six-foot buggy cue whip with no lash, and treats.

What you will be doing: You will be teaching your horse to keep his hindquarters turned away from you as you enter his stall.

How to proceed: Outfit yourself with your safety helmet, gloves, and boots. Remove from his stall, buckets and other things your horse could run into. Arm yourself with the six-foot buggy cue whip and an attitude of "How dare you threaten me!" Enter his box stall, keeping your arms down at

TRAINING KEY

Don't start a training session if you only have a few minutes to spend. If you have troubles, you cannot stop and finish it later. You must always finish a training session on a good note with the horse relaxed and yourself calm. Your horse will remember the last thing he did before you put him away. If he kicked you last and you put him away, he will think the act of kicking you is the quickest way to get you to leave him alone. Never end a session with the thought, "I don't have time to correct him now, but I'll do it tomorrow."

your sides, and call his name. It's best to keep his name to one syllable or use a short nickname. Say, "Tie, come." Praise him if he turns to you. Even if he just turns his head toward you, praise him. Try to stay positioned near the stall doorway so you won't get trapped in a corner should he decide to kick. You can stand in the middle of his stall only if it is large enough to do so and still keep out of his reach. If he turns tail, spank his rear end with the end of your whip. Use the same pressure as you would in lightly swatting a fly just above his tail. Your goal is to surprise him but not to hurt him.

A word of warning: Horses have an amazing reach both to the side and behind with their hind legs. Never allow yourself to come within kicking or striking range. Young adults or beginners should always have supervision or help when correcting a tail turner.

Stay well out of his reach. Most wild, scared, or mean horses will try to climb up the back corner of their stall in a desperate attempt to get away. No matter what happens, keep up your swats. It may help to count out the swats evenly. Some horses will put up a frantic attempt to get away and race around the stall. They may break into a sweat and even fall down. Remain calm and keep up your swats. Spank only his rear end just above his tail, and never strike at his head or legs. Do not keep up a running chatter. Keep quiet until he stops and looks at you.

It may not make sense to spank a horse that is fearful, thinking that it will instill more fear into him. At first it does. He tries to flee and finds that he cannot. He may panic and put up a real rodeo. When he discovers that you will not stop and he cannot get away, he will start to use his head. He will think that you are spanking him for no reason until he discovers that you will stop when he stops and faces you. That is when you show him you are pleased. Here is where your timing first comes into play. Watch his head, and the second he glances your way, drop your whip arm to your side or behind your back and praise him with your happy and soft voice. Heap on the praise, even using baby talk to show him your pleasure. You want him to stand with at least his head toward you. In the beginning he may only face you with his turned head and not his whole body, which is good for a start. Give him a few minutes to stand and catch his breath and praise him with words. Repeat the test. If he tries to flee, repeat the lesson until he turns his head to you. Many abused horses, or those with high opinions of themselves, will refuse to look at you. They may turn their head or body to face you but keep their eyes averted. They seem to say, "You can make me face you, but you can't make me look at you." Flick the end of your whip at your horse until he looks at you with his eyes. Praise him every time he looks at you, and flick the end of the whip when he looks away. You must be very clear on what pleases you and what does not. He needs to stop all movement with his feet and turn his head to look at you when you call him. You cannot accept his being almost correct. A horse that will not turn to look at you is not trying.

Every time you enter his stall, repeat the lesson if he turns tail. Each time he should turn to face you sooner. Your goal will be to enter his stall and call his name and have him turn to greet you. He may still be grumpy, but he will learn that it's safer for him to keep his rear end away from you. He will soon make the connection that you are happy with his face and unhappy with his tail and will spank him if he turns it toward you. You are becoming the leader, and he, the follower.

You should never take a few swings at him if he turns his

> **⚓ REMEMBER THIS TIP**
>
> Never start some-
> thing you cannot fin-
> ish. Half way correcting a
> bad behavior is sometimes
> worse than not at all.

tail toward you and then rattle the grain bucket to catch him. You will be training him it is all right to threaten you and even reward his behavior with food. You will end up with a spoiled horse that knows he can call your bluff. Bribing him with food will not give him the opportunity to use his brain and think. He will never get the opportunity to resist you and find out that it won't work.

It's a bit like never asking a horse that hates water to cross a river. As long as you never cross a river, you'll get along great. However, if you ask him to cross a river and he pitch-es a royal fit and you give in, you've taught him that he calls the shots. On the other hand, if you insist that he cross the river, he resists, and you still insist and make him cross the river, he'll learn that *you* call the shots.

Once you can approach him and he no longer turns his tail toward you, you can reward him with your happy voice, generous pats, and a good scratching of his favorite itchy spots. You want him to look forward to your visits and not just to the food you might be carrying.

Teaching Your Horse to Come to You

What you will need: Leg wraps, six-foot buggy cue whip, and treats.

What you will be doing: You will be teaching your horse to stop in one corner and turn his head toward you, first in his stall and then in a larger area. Once he learns to stop and face you, he will next learn to come to you.

You can continue the tail-turner correction training in a

larger enclosure after you have success in his stall. Many horses can be easily caught in small spaces but refuse to be caught in larger areas. This training can greatly help this type of horse. At first he may race around and ignore you in the wide-open spaces where your whip can no longer reach him. You can now teach him to use a safety corner. A safety corner is one corner of the arena that you have selected for him to stop in when asked. This is very helpful in correcting a horse that won't let you catch him. This method works best in a small area such as a round pen, training ring, or small indoor arena. Do not use a grassy pen, as he will be trying to snatch grass instead of paying attention to you.

How to proceed: Outfit yourself in your safety helmet, gloves, and boots. Let your horse loose in the pen and work him at liberty until he shows signs of tiring and wanting to stop. Select a corner to be his safety corner. Do not use a corner with a gate or you will be training him to run to the door. When he gets to the corner you have selected as his safety corner, ask him to stop. Use the same word firmly each time — "Whoa!" Now is not the time to hold a running conversation with him. You may have to cut him off and make him go back to the safety corner. Once there, let him stand and catch his breath for a few minutes. If he's not tired or ready to stop, he won't appreciate the rest you are offering him. He will probably turn tail to you or stand facing the corner.

Send him around again at a steady pace for several rounds and then tell him to whoa again when he nears his safety corner. If he refuses to stop, send him on again. Keep his feet moving at a brisk pace. He gets no rest for not responding correctly.

It's a game to him until he learns that it isn't fun anymore and he'd like to stop and rest. Soon, he will be glad to stop when you ask. If the area is too large, he will run to one end and stop while you run after him. Watching you run while he rests is great sport for him. If your only option is a large arena, enlist a friend to stand at the other end. The two of you can keep him moving

REMEMBER THIS TIP

The secret is to make him go a little faster and a little longer than he wants. Make him huff and puff a little. You want him looking to you for the signal that he may stop. The decision is yours and not his.

at a fast trot or canter until you ask him to whoa. Once he stops and stands in his corner, he should turn his head to you. Be sure to keep your whip down and behind you when you ask him to stop.

When he turns and looks at you, repeat the praise that you gave in his stall. He will learn that even though your whip can't reach him in a larger area, you can still control him. You are the leader, and he is doing all the footwork until you tell him when and where to stop. His reward is to receive a rest break and praise in his safety corner. As long as he still faces you, you can approach him and give him a treat there if you like. With your whip arm down and behind you, talk to him softly as you approach him. If he runs away, repeat the lesson by making him go faster and longer than he wants to. Ask him again to whoa when he's near his corner. Your goal is for him to go to his corner and face you.

Once he is stopped in his safety corner, you can teach him to come to you by calling his name. Keep your arms and whip down or behind you. Encourage him to take a few steps toward you. In the beginning you can walk up to meet him and praise and reward him. As you repeat this scenario, he should take more and more steps toward you. Your goal now is to have him stop in his safety corner when asked and to come to you when called.

Eventually, as he comes to you, you should be able to turn and walk away and he will follow you. If he starts to follow you and then runs off, repeat the lesson of making him go faster and longer than he wanted.

Ask him to come to you again and to follow you, but don't do anything that would threaten him. Keep your cue whip down or behind your back. Always give him praise and rest when he comes to you. It is fun to see this method work and to watch his expression as he figures it out. You can actually watch his eyes soften and his lips relax.

The first few weeks can go smoothly or be filled with his frantic attempts to run away. Repeat the lessons until he has mastered stopping in his safety corner when you ask, turning his head to look at you, coming when you call, and following you without a lead rope. When he does what is asked, you can praise him by rubbing his forehead until he relaxes and drops his head. His reward is that you have quit making him work, he can relax and rest, and he gets a treat.

Never repeat a good movement over and over or you will be punishing him for good work. You want him to understand that if he responds correctly you will reward him with praise, food, and rest.

Troubleshooting: Keep your whip up, about four feet off the ground, when asking him to keep moving. When you want him to stop, drop your whip arm down to your side or behind you. Don't approach him with your whip up or in front of you. You horse will interpret the raised whip or arm as a threat, and he'll move off. When he stops and faces you, drop your whip arm and praise him. Be sure to smile and be happy when he does well.

> ### ♋ REMEMBER THIS TIP
>
> Your horse would rather relax in his stall and do nothing. When you get a good response to your training, praise him and put him away. He will do more learning in his stall after your training session than he will while you are working with him. He will return to his stall and think.

Nothing is more rewarding than teaching an ornery horse that has refused to be caught for years how to come to you. He starts out so smug and self-satisfied with the idea that he is going to make you chase him from one end of the ring to the other. He prances around just out of reach. As you near him, he takes off for a fun game of "Catch Me If You Can." You can almost see a smile on his face as he gives you a backward glance over his shoulder. He makes you either want to cry or shoot him! It is just delightful to see him transform into a horse that will actually drop his head and come to you looking for rest, comfort, and a rub on his forehead.

Teaching to Give to Pressure

What you will need: A stable halter, lead rope with chain, and treats.

What you will be doing: You will be teaching your horse to give to pressure placed on the bridge of his nose. When you cue him, he will drop his head and keep it there.

How to proceed: Outfit yourself with your safety helmet, gloves, and boots. Put a halter on your horse. Place a short lead rope with a short chain over his nose. You can wrap it once around the halter noseband to protect a sensitive nose. However, the training will be more effective if the chain goes directly over his nose. Many people baby and pamper their horse. They use a very mild bit and then can't control the

animal. The horse practically pulls their arms out of
their sockets before he'll
stop. While no one wants
to be cruel to his horse,
what is the animal being
taught? He is being taught
that it's okay to jerk and
pull his trainer.

REMEMBER THIS TIP

By chasing him and
making him work, he
will come to you for rest
and comfort (the opposite
of what you would expect).
You have now taught him
to come to you.

Cruelty is in the control of the trainer. A snaffle bit is usually a mild bit unless a fool constantly jerks on his horse's
mouth with it. A chain over the nose is more severe than one
snapped to the halter ring, but your horse will learn it is
unpleasant to pull against you. You can develop fingertip
control over him rather than bracing yourself with both
hands for the dragging match he could give you. There is no
need to hurt your horse, but he must be respectful of you
and your wishes.

Stand beside his left shoulder facing forward. Gently tug
the lead rope in short little tugs while pulling down slightly.
He will normally try to raise his head and pull against the
pressure. Do not try to pull his head down. Keep your hand
steady and keep up your little tugs. Use the same pressure
you would playing "Pat-a-Cake" with a baby. The horse may
resist by pulling up or jerking away from you. Watch him
closely. The second you see him give to the pressure and put
his head down, stop tugging. Here is your good timing
again. Praise him. Loosen the chain and rub his nose where
the chain crossed over it. Pat his forehead and speak kindly
to him for a few minutes.

Repeat the tugging until he drops his head again. It may be
half an inch, but stop and praise him. Horses love to hear

praise and get love strokes. Show your excitement over how much this means to you. Remember helping a baby learn to walk? Go ahead and sound like a fool. Only your horse can hear you.

Repeat this exercise daily until you can get your horse to drop his head to any level and hold it there for 30 to 60 seconds. Spend a few minutes each day until you both have mastered this before moving on. This is the first major step in teaching your horse submission, giving to pressure, and the beginning of what he needs to know to start his trick training. This training will benefit your horse his entire life. You can also use a cue word that you can repeat each time you ask him to lower his head. It will be helpful when bridling him, braiding his mane, treating injuries, or perhaps helping him to free himself from entrapments such as ropes or fencing.

✂ REMEMBER THIS TIP

Most horses must be taught to give or to move away from pressure. If not taught this, they will lean into or pull against any type of pressure.

One of my horses caught his halter ring on the door latch on my horse trailer. He panicked and pulled back, and no one was brave enough to get close enough to try and free him. Someone came and got me. I told the horse his cue word, he dropped his head, and the ring slipped off the latch. This horse is a very high-strung Arabian, but he remembered his training, listened when he most needed to, and quite possibly saved himself from serious injury.

As you become more advanced with your horse's training, you can teach him to drop his head from hand or leg cues when he's being ridden. While sitting on his back, hold the reins just tightly enough that he cannot step forward and

Apply light downward tugs until he lowers his head.

Eventually he should drop his head and keep it down as long as asked.

bump him with both your legs at his girth area. At the same time jiggle the reins just to encourage him to drop his head. When his head drops, stop bumping him with your legs and release the reins. His reward is that you will immediately release the pressure on his mouth and sides when he drops his head. With practice you can teach him to drop his head from just a light leg and hand cue — so slight the judge will never notice. This training will greatly benefit your show horses. In trail classes you can earn extra points by subtly cue-ing your horse to drop his head to look briefly at an obstacle before he crosses it, if he doesn't do it on his own. A show horse must carry his head in a relaxed and "breed correct" position. Should something along the rail scare him, his head will pop up out of position. If you have trained your horse to drop his head, he will respond by dropping his head and relaxing instead of lifting it to focus on the spooky object. If he becomes more alarmed, he might spook off the rail. His giving-to-pressure training will remind him to focus his attention back on you and off the object. A horse cannot be tense with his head down.

A horse that travels with his head up or one that constantly flips his head up in resistance to rein pressure will usually have a hollow back, which makes for a rough ride and causes his hind legs to trail behind him. The overall picture is one of resistance, roughness, and lack of balance and collection.

A horse that gives to rein and leg pressure will travel with an arched neck and back, will be a smoother ride because of his arched back, and will be able to get his hind legs under himself for better impulsion. He will be more comfortable and collected, making for a happier horse and rider. The overall picture is one of balance and collection.

When you feel your show horse start to come off the bit and tense up over something unusual along the rail, a simple squeeze of the leg and a jiggling of the rein can cause him to drop his head and stay in position. You can catch a problem long before it happens if you have correctly trained your horse and honed your skills at reading and feeling his body language. You and he will have become one!

Moving Away From Pressure

What you will need: Halter, short lead rope with chain, leg wraps, dressage-length cue whip, and treats.

What you will be doing: You will be building on your horse's first lessons by now asking him to step sideways away from your cue whip.

How to proceed: Outfit yourself with your safety helmet, gloves, and boots. Halter your horse and equip him with a lead rope. Place the chain over his nose. You can make the chain less harsh by wrapping it once or twice around the halter noseband. Stand with your back against a fence or arena wall with your horse at a 90-degree angle to the wall and facing it. Do not stand directly in front of him. Should he become frustrated and try to strike at you, you want to be off to the side slightly out of his striking zone.

Start by asking him to step sideways to his right. Tap his left side with your cue whip. Hold your whip parallel to the ground and in the middle of his body. Try to get his entire body to move sideways and not just his shoulders or hindquarters. Most untrained horses will step into the whip instead of away from it. You're asking him to move, but he may not know where to move to, so he may try several different directions before the correct one. If he tries to step forward, the wall will stop him. If he steps back you can pull him back up to the wall again. Keep tapping his side lightly until he steps away from the whip to his right. Pour on the praise. Stroke his forehead and let him relax. Most horses will step to the right easier than stepping to the left, which is why we teach moving to the right first. In addition, most people are right-handed, which makes controlling the cue whip easier if held in the right hand. Repeat the taps asking him to step right. A cue word such as "over" can be used. A few steps are a good start. Give him time to understand what you are asking for and praise him for any good response.

A word of warning: Many horses will often try to bite the arm that's holding the lead rope. Your arm is right under the horse's nose, so it's very tempting for him to bite it in a moment of frustration. Keep an eye on his mouth as you first teach this lesson. Wearing some additional padding on your arm is preferable to having bare arms. Should he attempt to bite, jerk the lead and shout "No!" Make it clear that this is very unacceptable behavior and he will be punished for any biting attempt. Even a small pinch to your arm from a colt hurts, so consider all bites, no matter how small, unacceptable. It's not your job to duck and dive out of his reach. It's his job to behave himself and be a gentleman at all times. Almost all young horses will try biting your arm at least once during this lesson so be prepared for it and don't be surprised. A quick punishment, followed by a moment to settle down, followed by repeating the moving-away-from-pressure lesson, is usually effective in discouraging any biting. Your horse will learn that biting will not make you stop his training. Should he bite and you stop and put him away, you will be giving him what he wants and reinforcing the idea that it's okay to bite you. He will be quicker to take a snatch at you next time if he got away with a bite in your last session. Be ready for a possible bite and correct it as soon as it happens.

Should he attempt a cow kick sideways at the whip, make it clear that kicking is not acceptable either and repeat the tapping. He will soon learn that he can try to bite, kick, rear, pull away, or even fall down and you will not stop until he does what you ask. When he complies, reward him with rest. Keep your cool, relax your body language, and don't appear threatening or intimidating to your horse. You are only asking him to step away from a light tap on his side, which shouldn't be too much to ask. When you get the response you want, be quick to show your horse how pleased you are. Praise him with your body language, voice, a possible treat, and loving strokes to his head and neck. Take him on a short walk around the arena for a few minutes then repeat the training. If he steps off easily in the direction you want, praise him and put him away. Repeat again the following day and ask for stepping away from the whip in either direction. He may get stuck and move the wrong direction a time or two, but remain relaxed and keep working with him until he's easily moving off the whip pressure in either direction for longer and longer distances. Don't overwork him by continually repeating the lesson or

making him go too far after he starts to do it well. He will begin to think you are punishing him for doing what you ask of him. Working up to 20 feet in each direction is enough. In following training sessions, ask him to step over a few times in each direction each day and then put him away or move on to something else.

Once he is moving away easily, try side passing him, in hand, over a ground pole or log. This movement can also easily be cued from the saddle with just your leg pressure. The horse should move away from your leg and step to the side. Once he steps to the side, release your leg pressure. This move will be very helpful in show-ring trail classes or on real trail rides. A horse that doesn't worry about things under and around his legs is a blessing on the trail. Should you get into a tricky situation on the trail, it's wonderful just to ask your horse to step to the side to avoid the problem and he responds in a quiet and trusting way. Your friends will envy your training abilities and wish they were riding your horse.

The time you spend teaching your horse to give to pressure

has many benefits. He will be able to round up and collect himself more easily. He will be able to bend his frame in the corners of the ring in your pleasure classes, rather than being stiff and unyielding as a board. And he will be able to side pass objects on the ground in a trail class or on a trail ride with just slight leg pressure from his rider.

4

Teaching Your Horse to Bow

I like to start trick training by teaching the bow. It can be either easy or very difficult to teach, depending on how smart your horse is and how well you can teach it.

The bow has several steps. With ropes to hold and hooves to avoid, it can prove challenging for both horse and trainer to understand at first. But if you can master teaching him this trick, you will prove to yourself that you can succeed at trick training.

In addition to practicing each step of the trick thoroughly, teaching the bow requires good timing, effective body language, and sometimes even physical strength from you.

Remember, you get out of it what you put into it. If trick training were so easy, everyone would have a trick horse. You will have already taught him to give to pressure and drop his head. The bow is the natural extension of these lessons. You will be putting together a trick from a simple series of earlier submissions. Once your horse understands what you are asking and gives to the pressure and does so in a relaxed frame of mind and body, he is ready to learn more. Now, let's get going!

What you will need: Halter, lead rope with chain, leg wraps, 15-foot soft rope with a loop in one end, and treats. You may have to vary the length of the rope, depending on the size of your horse. Twenty feet should be long enough for a large Quarter Horse; 12, for a large pony.

What you will be doing: You will be teaching your horse to accept a rope lifting and holding up his right front leg. With his leg held up, he will drop his head, shift his weight to his hindquarters, and bow down on his right front cannon bone.

How to proceed: Put a halter and leg wraps on your horse. Be sure to outfit yourself with your safety helmet, boots, and leather gloves. Lead your horse to your work area. Since your horse will be kneeling on the ground, be sure that the area is extra soft and free from stones. Bed the area with deep sawdust, shavings, or straw if the ground is even slightly hard. Sand can be abrasive and irritating to eyes and ears, so be careful even when working in sand indoor arenas that look soft. Check your horse often for any signs of abrasions or scrapes. If you find any, make your work area bedding deeper and softer. Do not bed the area in hay or work in an area of deep grass as he might focus all his attention on eating it!

Be sure that your training area is free from anything in which your horse may become entangled, such as wire fenc-

TRAINING KEY

Before you begin, be sure that you aren't starting your training just before your horse's usual dinnertime. If he's hungry or all his horse pals are eating and he isn't, he will not be focused on you. You also don't want to wait until he's just eaten, as no one wants to work just after dinner, and treats won't be as appealing. You want him a little bit hungry but not starving. Also, don't turn all his stablemates out in the pasture, leaving him behind. Otherwise, his attention will be outside and not on you.

ing and gates. Tie up any loose dogs and shoo away the spectators. If your horse has never been in your work area before, lead him around in it until he relaxes. His head should drop when you ask him, and his jaw and lips should be

relaxed. If he is too nervous to eat a treat, he is not ready to learn and you'll need to take more time with him. If he seems relaxed and happy, you're ready to start.

Take your 15-foot soft, non-stretchy rope and lay it across his back a few times. Walk him around and let the ends drag on the ground. He should be relaxed and not be worried about the dangling rope. If he tries to spook away from the rope or looks worried about it, take more time to desensitize him to it. Once he is calm and worry free, take the rope off and make a small, non-slip running loop in one end. Run the free end of the rope through the loop until you have a sliding loop in one end. (See Appendix for a step-by-step guide to making a running loop.)

Slip this loop over your horse's right front ankle just above his hoof. You should now have a sliding loop that will be easy to remove when you need to and will not slip down into a tight knot. Run the rest of the rope up and over his back, just behind his withers where your saddle would sit. Now you will have the rope up and over his back with one end looped around his right front ankle and the other end touching the ground on his left side. Stand beside his left shoulder and pull the rope until his right cannon bone is parallel with the ground.

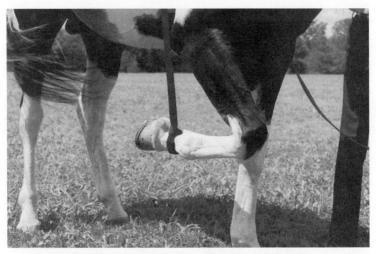

Slip the loop over the horse's right front ankle.

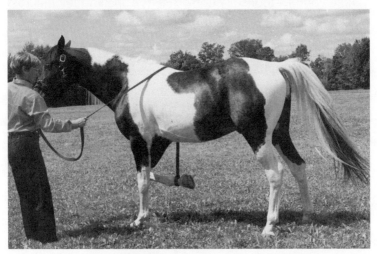

Run the rest of the rope up and over his back.

No matter what, don't let him pull the rope out of your hand so he can put his right hoof back on the ground. Let him think that you are stronger than he is. The only way he can get his leg back on the ground is to bow down on his cannon bone. Only when he bows will you give him back his leg.

He should *not* think that the fastest way to regain control of all four of his feet is to pitch enough of a fit that you will give up and return him to his stall. To regain control of his feet, get his reward, and be returned to his stall depend 100 percent on his cooperation and obedience to your cues. This takes time, but the "light will come on" and your horse will start to understand after a few training sessions.

Depending on your horse's temperament, the first time you use the rope to pull up his leg might be a difficult moment. He might just stand there looking confused. Young and nervous horses might hop around on three legs or even give you a rodeo. *Never* hold the rope so you can't let go in an emergency and *never* wrap the rope around your hand. Do not tie the rope in a knot because you will not be able to release his leg quickly when he does bow. In an emergency it's always okay to let go of the leg rope. It might set your training back a bit, but that's better than getting either you or your horse injured. Should he surprise you with a leap into the air or a flip over backward, let go of the rope. I have worked with so many horses that I can gauge their body language and can be one step ahead of their next movement. I can see a leap coming and just go with it. If a horse wants to pitch a fit, I can move with him in his vain attempt to pull free. However, a beginner trick trainer will not have the knowledge to keep control in this type of situation. It's better for the trainer to get out of the way, and when the horse has calmed, try again. If your horse is a gentle ol' soul, he should calmly let you lift his leg up to a 90-degree angle. He should already know how to drop his head down from learning how to give his head to pressure in his earlier lesson.

Next you will ask him to drop his head while you are holding his leg up with the rope. To do this, you need to pull

down and back on his lead rope with your left hand. You will
be facing the horse's shoulder near his left elbow. Don't pull
too hard on the halter, as you don't want this to become the
cue for the bow, which will eventually be a tap with the
whip behind his right knee. Pull the lead rope toward the
ground or his chest. A pull to the side could twist his head
around to the side and make him topple over and lie down.
He should try to respond to this cue if you have correctly
taught him to lower his head and hold it there. He should
lower his head and give to the down and rearward pressure.
Ideally, he should shift his weight to the rear and kneel
down on his right front leg. If he hasn't quite gotten the
idea, lean your right hip into his left shoulder and try to
push him to his right and back. Or, use your left hand, which
is holding the lead rope, to push into his shoulder pressure
point. Press your hand into the groove in front of his shoulder, halfway between his withers and the point of his shoulder, and press on the muscle you can feel there, to encourage him to shift his weight rearward. Push your horse over

Ask the horse to lower his head and shift his weight to the rear.

and back all in one smooth motion while keeping his right front leg up with the leg rope. His cannon bone, not his knee, should lie flat on the ground.

The moment his cannon bone touches the ground, release the rope, let him stand up on all four legs, and praise him. Show him exactly how thrilled you are with him. Stroke him, dance around, and clap. Let him know that clapping and praise are good things and not something to fear. Reward him with a treat and put him away. Once is enough for his first attempt. Should you get a fairly decent bow, repeating the trick would be punishment. His reward is the treat, your praise, and rest. He will soon figure out that if he works with you instead of against you, he will find reward and rest sooner.

Repeat this exercise daily until your horse easily bows when you lift his leg with the rope and give him the halter pull cues of down and back. This may take days, weeks, or even months. Remember that your first horse will be the hardest to train, and it takes both patience and skill to mas-

Once the cannon bone touches the ground, release the rope.

ter teaching even simple tricks. Some horses are so relaxed that learning tricks is simple for them. For others that are nervous and fearful, this is asking much of them. To them you are confining them with ropes, pulling in several directions, and seemingly asking for several different things at the

TRAINING KEY

It is very important that you do not pull his hoof up to his belly, as this will make him kneel down on his kneecap instead of his cannon bone. All of his weight down on his knee will be painful, and he won't want to repeat the bow for you.

same time. They might try to fight you at first, but often these horses make the best trick horses in the end. Each horse is an individual, and some horses are quicker to submit and try to understand what their human is telling them.

For your second training session, again use the rope to get your horse to bow. When he does, release the rope, reward him, and walk him around a few minutes. Do not repeat the bow more than three times per session, with short, relaxing walks in between.

Once your horse is bowing well with the rope (perhaps in five training sessions if he is a quick learner and longer if he is not), drop the leg rope and try tapping him behind his right front knee with your dressage-length cue whip while repeating the halter cues. Keep tapping behind his right front knee to keep him holding that leg up, while giving him his halter cue of down and back. If he doesn't respond correctly, go back to the leg rope for a while longer. If he still doesn't seem to understand, try lifting his right leg with the rope while holding a treat under his nose. Bring the treat back and down and he should move his weight to the rear and relax down onto his leg as he attempts to follow it. Allow him to eat his reward while still in the bowing position. This will teach him to stay down longer, rather than to bow quickly and then pop to his feet to look for his reward. The longer you can keep him down the better. In the beginning, if he can hold the position for just a few moments, that's fine as the bow is difficult to hold. Remember, your horse will not want to perform the bow if it's painful to his muscles, knees, and joints. As he develops the muscles and the control to bow, it will become much easier for him. As he progresses further, once again try using just the whip cue behind the right knee while repeating the halter cues. While still holding his lead rope in your left hand, hold a treat, also in the same hand, and show him that you have it by touching his nose with it. As he reaches for it, move it down and back. He should shift his weight to the rear, drop his head down and follow the treat, and bow down on his leg. A handful of oats should keep him down on his cannon bone while he eats.

Some people teach the bow by *just* holding a treat under a horse's nose and slowly moving the treat down and back until the horse grabs it. While it's okay to use a "tease carrot" or treat now and then, like described above, your whole training method should not be based on waving food under your horse's nose.

I want the horse to learn to give to pressure placed on him and not to fear ropes and entanglement, as submission to them could save his life in an unexpected situation. Food cues alone do not teach submission. Many a horse has broken his neck or legs in a blind panic. Anything I can do that teaches my horse to avoid injury is worthwhile.

Troubleshooting: If once the leg is raised with the rope and your horse just stands there and refuses to try to bow, try pushing your weight against his shoulder. Sometimes you have to show him physically what you want him to do. Push his shoulder blade away from you and to the rear. This will push him off balance, and he'll have to move. He may hop around, but just be ready to move with him. Praise him when he lowers his head when cued and push against him while his head is lowered. He may have to move his hind legs back to give himself room to bow, which is desirable.

If your horse leaps and jumps and you can't hold the leg rope, in addition to running the rope from his ankle over his back, run it under his belly and around itself once just above his lifted hoof and back toward you under his belly. This will give you the necessary strength to keep his leg raised. If he starts leaping, his back will take the weight of his leg instead of you struggling to keep his leg up.

This will also fix the problem of the rope slipping up his neck when he puts his head down to bow. You will still be holding the end of the rope in your right hand and his lead rope in your left while he makes some jumps around you in his attempt to free his leg. Should he make some tremendous leaps, just go with him. Keep your feet out of his way as he struggles. He may accidentally trip himself and fall. If he does, let go of the rope and let him regain his feet. Lead him around for a few minutes and be sure that he's relaxed before trying again. To him, he may fear being off his feet where he would be at the mercy of predators. Show him it's all right to bow down and get back up by calmly handling the situation. Soon he will give up the struggling and start paying attention to your halter cues. Praise him for any shift in weight to the rear and any attempt to bow. A very nervous horse may be sweating and upset at this point. Remain calm and con-

Running the rope under his belly provides more leverage.

tinue with the halter cues until he at least attempts a bow. Praise him and put him away. Try again later after he's had time to think about the task. You should think about the training session as well. Review the cues you gave him. The problem could be your body position, a too tight or too loose hold on the rope, too hard of a work surface, or not enough human muscle to push against him to show him which direction you are trying to get him to go. Never lose your temper and punish him. Horses, like people, vary in intelligence. Some are natural performers, and others have four left feet. Your horse's enjoyment in trick training is a direct reflection of how well you communicate what you want him to do.

I had a yearling colt that took months to figure out how to bow. I pushed and pulled and could eventually get him to bow with the leg rope, but he just couldn't comprehend what to do when I took the rope off. Rather than giving up, I just kept at it until one day he did it. I figured that it was just an accident, as he hadn't really been paying attention.

If the horse leaps, go with him.

A push helps shift his weight to the rear, but he is bracing.

He had just been allowing me to push and pull him around while he was more interested in watching the birds fly in and out of the barn. My actions didn't seem to mean anything to him. Then, all of a sudden, it clicked! I could see a complete change in the look in his eye — he had understood all my pushing meant something! He finally understood

The horse begins to understand and starts to lower his head.

what I was trying to do, and he woke up and started paying attention. From then on he could bow without the rope and was hungry to learn more. It must be akin to when children first learn to ask for something they want. At first they cry, then they cry and point, and then they learn to ask for it in words and you respond. It must be a thrilling moment when they learn to bridge that communication gap. It's the same with horses when you can bridge that same gap and ask your horse to do something and he understands.

Each day repeat your bowing training until your horse quickly bows down with just a tap behind his right knee. A series of light taps behind his knee will encourage him to stay down longer. Sometimes a horse will become so relaxed performing a bow that he will lie down. You will want him to lie down later so don't punish him for the mistake. If he is so relaxed that it was easy for him to lie down, count your blessings as teaching him to lie down is going to be a breeze. You want him to know that it's all right to lie down, but since you hadn't asked him for it, get him back up and repeat the bow

The bow is easily done under saddle by tapping the horse behind his right knee.

correctly before giving him any treats or praise.

The bow is easily done under saddle by tapping the horse behind his right knee with the dressage-length cue whip, until he drops his head and bows down on his right leg. You must be careful because when his front end drops down, your weight is thrown forward and it's easy to fall off over his head. Trust me — I know as I've done it myself! Sit back in the saddle so you will stay in balance when he bows.

Some people teach a horse to bow on his left front leg, and the cue is a tap behind the left knee as the trainer leans over in a bow himself. It looks quite nice in front of a crowd since it looks like horse and handler are both taking a bow together. However, horses that are trained this way sometimes bow at unexpected moments. The farrier bends over to lift the horse's left front hoof, and the horse bows! You get off to pick up a dropped article and the horse bows.

Once you have trained a few horses, you'll be able to read

their body language better and will be better prepared for their first reactions to being restrained. There are other ways to make a horse bow. You could tie up a leg and tire him enough that he falls down on his knees or "lace" his legs with a whip until he drops down on his knees, but what is he learning? These methods will not make for a willing and happy performer, and he will learn to fear you and your cue whip. Your cue whip is just an extension of your hand and not for punishment or intimidation.

You want your horse to use his head. It's okay for him to fight a little if he feels he has to try it, but it isn't going to help him get away, or avoid the task at hand. Only when he uses his head and relaxes will he find reward and rest. Just knocking a horse off his feet will not teach him anything but pain and fear of you. Actually, if he struggles with the rope and finds that he can't get away, he will learn faster. You have shown him that you are stronger than he is and can make him submit to your wishes gently. When he does submit, you will praise him and put him away. Once your horse understands this, he will learn other tricks more easily. All tricks are performed by asking for some form of submission and relaxation of the horse's muscles. You start slowly, establish a base, and build all tricks from that base. The sky and your imagination are the limits.

5

Teaching Your Horse to Lie Down

Once your horse has mastered the bow, you both will be ready to move on to lying down. This trick will be the most difficult for your horse to learn thus far, because you will be asking for a series of different moves. Since part of the lying-down cues stem from the bow cues and responses, he must fully understand how to drop his head, lean his weight to the rear, and bow down on one knee easily.

What you will need: Halter, lead rope, leg wraps, fifteen-foot soft rope with a running loop in one end, and treats. You may have to vary the length of the rope, depending on the size of your horse.

What you will be doing: You will be teaching your horse the maximum in relaxation and submission by asking him to lie down.

How to proceed: Outfit yourself with your safety helmet, gloves, and boots. Take your horse to your training spot, which should be heavily bedded with soft material. Be sure to wrap all four legs. Ask your horse to bow in the usual way. Once he is bowing, pull his head around to his left side and push your weight into his left shoulder. If he is relaxed, you will feel his muscles soften, and he'll fall easily onto his side. Your horse will be slightly confused since you have

Once the horse is in a bowing position, tap behind his left knee until he folds both legs under himself.

Keep tapping his cue spot until he lies down.

asked him for a bow and he bowed for you. However, to him, now you aren't happy with that, and now you want him to do something else. If you are slow and careful in your training, he will begin to understand that you are trying to teach him something new, and he'll try his best to understand. A series of taps behind his right knee will encourage him to stay down should he try to stand back up.

Troubleshooting: If he will only bow and then try to hop back up to his feet, go back to the training rope. With the rope you will be able to keep him from getting his foot back. He'll have to bow, and with enough time and your help in pushing his body over, he should relax enough to lie down. Once he is down, release the leg rope and praise and reward him. When you want him to rise, pull up on the lead rope and say, "Get up." Put him away.

For the right leg bow, cue your horse to bow by tapping him behind his right knee. Once he is in the bowing position, pull his head around to his left slightly and give him a series of taps behind his left elbow until he lies down. Horses just learning how to lie down on cue most often lie down from the one-legged bow. When they become more skilled and confident, they usually will switch to lying down from a both-knees-down position, as it's more comfortable for them.

The exception would be an older horse with arthritis or any horse with an injury that would make lying down, or getting up, painful. If you have a horse such as that, it would be best to skip teaching him to lie down.

Since horses are prey animals, many don't feel safe while lying down. You must be sure to give your horse the confidence to believe it's safe to lie down. Make sure that he won't get hurt or scrape the hair off his hide, and once he is down, make sure he receives plenty of praise and rewards. Plus, he will realize he can return to his stall that much sooner. The goal is to keep him relaxed enough to lie down and stay there a few minutes. Feed him his treats when he is lying down to encourage him to stay down. Give him another treat after you ask him to stand up. If you just reward after he gets up, he will think the reward is for getting up and not for lying down. Give two rewards for two separate things.

A word of warning: Many a horse will lie down only to pop quickly back up to his feet. Be sure that your own feet are out of his way. He will have to throw his head up, his front feet out in front, and then push off with his hind feet to get up. It's easy to get a mashed toe. Don't let yourself be so close to him when he gets up; either you'll be in his way or tangled up in his legs.

It is often more difficult to get the horse to lie down on his second day of training. He may have learned to spread his hind feet and brace himself enough that you can't push him over. If he braces, you can push your shoulder into his side enough to make him move one of his back feet so that he can no longer brace against your pushing him over. You might have to push farther back into his flank with your hip to get him to relax his hind feet — you might have to do this several times. If his muscles are tense, he is resisting lying down. Softly tell him to lie down, relax, there's a good boy, down, down, down to help calm his fears. About this point he may think you have gone nuts. You are pushing and pulling on him and he just holds his ground. Make sure that the bedding is extra soft and that animals and people are not around to distract him. If people keep popping in the door asking how you're doing, he's not going to be relaxed, focused on you, or be willing to take the chance of lying down. Sometimes it helps if he's a little hot and itchy and the idea of lying down for a good roll sounds pretty appealing.

Once he does lie down, try not to let him roll. You don't want to establish the habit especially should you ever ask your horse to lie down with a saddle on him. When he rolls up on his back to attempt to roll, tap him on his belly and tell him "No." When he's quietly lying up on his chest, praise and reward him. Gently stroke his neck and back.

Regardless of whether you want your horse to lie on his chest or his side, you need to start with him lying on his chest. Horses feel very insecure lying flat on their sides. Once you have gotten your horse to where he will easily lie down on his chest, you can encourage him to roll onto his side. If he relaxes and rolls over, praise him. If he seems afraid to try it, don't worry. Try again after he becomes more advanced and comfortable in lying down and staying there.

After he begins to understand how to lie down, you should be able to tap him behind the back of his right knee until he bows. Then, tap him behind his left knee until he folds that under so he's bowing on both front legs. Then, ask him to lie down by lightly tapping him just under his left elbow until he lies down.

Nothing can make your horse lie down unless he wants to, so always try to make the learning experience an enjoyable one for him. Expect your first training sessions to be awkward, but they will get smoother with time and practice. Never punish your horse for doing wrong. Simply do not reward him until you get the behavior that you want from him.

Be sure you use the same cues and do not confuse your horse with mixed signals and ill-timed rewards. Always remember to praise him for the correct response. Clap, smile, and tell him how good he is, in addition to giving him his food reward.

Troubleshooting: If you simply cannot make him even try to lie down by having him bow and pulling his head around to

There are many variations of this trick...

...including standing on the horse.

the left, try pulling his head around to the right with the lead rope run over the top of his right shoulder. In this way his body will fall toward you instead of away from you. When he lies down, his feet will face away from you, which is a slightly safer way for him to lie down. You won't get stepped on as easily when he gets up.

A word of warning: You can also teach your horse to lie down under saddle. It will be your job to determine which side he will be lying down on and to get your leg out of the way. If you pull his head slightly to the right, his body should go down to the left. He could easily accidentally lie down on your leg or foot. It will also be your job to watch his body language and not allow him to roll. He could catch your leg under him or damage the saddle if he rolls. If your horse is hot and itchy, the idea of a good roll will be very appealing to him. You also must not allow him to catch a hoof in the stirrup.

6

Standing on a Box

Compared to more difficult tricks such as bowing and lying down, standing on a box seems very simple. You just lead your horse to a box and have him step up onto it. For some horses it *is* just that easy. For other horses it is a monumental moment when they can conquer their fears, tentatively step up onto a small box with all four feet, and teeter there. To master this trick, your horse will have to develop the confidence to approach and step up onto the box when cued. He will also need the patience to hold that position and, as the box gets smaller and taller, the muscle control to gather all four feet underneath himself and balance there.

Learning to stand on a smaller-sized box seems to be a turning point in many trick horses' training. Many horses seem to be just going through the motions until they understand the box trick. From that point on, many become "hungry" to learn more. I've seen many a wild colt's eye permanently soften the moment he understands this trick. It's as if he says, "Oh, I've got it! You weren't just being an idiot pushing and pulling me around. You were trying to teach me something. Now, what else can we do?" This is the precise reason we teach tricks.

What you will need: Halter, lead rope with a chain, leg wraps, a sheet of plywood, a strong, safe wooden box for your horse to stand on, and treats.

What you will be doing: You will be teaching your horse first to accept walking on a sheet of plywood to accustom him to the sound and feel of it. When he has mastered that, you will be asking him to step up onto a wooden box.

How to proceed: Outfit yourself in your hard hat, gloves, and boots. Lead your horse onto the sheet of plywood you've placed in your training area. Stop him; then praise and reward him. To an older, well-trained horse this will be simple.

However, to a horse that has never been asked to come near, and then step onto, unfamiliar objects, this might be a time-consuming movement. It is a horse's nature to back away from unusual objects and look at them from a distance and all sides before approaching any closer. Your horse must be able to step calmly onto the plywood, stand for however long you want him to, and calmly step off, before you can start teaching him to stand on a box. Lead him up to the plywood and cue him to drop his head to look at it. Encourage him to touch the plywood. Reward him if he is able to approach the plywood and stand his ground near it. When he stands calmly next to the plywood, lead him forward onto it. Spend as much time as it takes to teach him to accept the sound and feel of the plywood before you go on. The larger the sheet of plywood you start with, the easier it will be for the fearful horse. Reduce the size as he becomes accepting and is no longer trying to evade the wood by stepping around it or jumping over it. If the plywood is slippery, tack a piece of carpeting or spread a few handfuls of sand on it for improved traction.

A word of warning: Be aware that your horse might jump onto, or off of, the plywood. Do not stand in front of him as you lead him across.

Once your horse becomes accustomed to the plywood, you can introduce the box. You must use a tip-proof, non-slippery, horse-strength, solid box built from strong, thick wood. You wouldn't ask your horse to do something that could injure him, so never ask him to stand on anything that he could tip over, fall though, slip off, or trap a leg in. In the beginning, the larger and closer to the ground the box is, the better. Depending on the size and weight of your horse, he may need a custom-designed starter box to fit him best. Keep in mind not to make the box too heavy if it is to be moved often. Low boxes can be square since they are less likely to tip if a horse stands on the edge of one. As you increase the height, the base should be wider than the top for added safety. For the average-sized horse, if you intend him to be able to stand on it with all four feet, a 36-inch by 36-inch box at about a foot off the ground is a good starter size. (See Appendix for instructions on building your own box.) You want to set your horse up for success by making standing on the box as easy as possible for him.

You can reduce the size of the box and increase its height, to say 26 by 26 inches wide and 15 to 18

Ask the horse to place one foot in the center of the box.

inches high for your second box, when your horse becomes more advanced. (The box used in the series of photos is 26 by 26 inches wide and 10 inches tall.) How small you can make the box depends on the size of your horse.

Obviously, the smaller your box, the more difficult it will be for him to get all four of his feet balanced on it. Don't reduce the box size too quickly just to impress your friends. It is more important to build a bond of trust between yourself and your horse than to impress anyone.

It is usually easier to get your horse to stand on a box if it's up against a solid wall like the side of your indoor arena or practice ring. If you are standing on his left, place the box close to a wall so the horse's right side will be against the wall. This prevents the horse from walking around one side of the box to evade stepping on it. As your horse advances to placing all four feet on the box, the wall will help him not to swing his haunches off the side of the box.

Let your horse thoroughly smell the box. Put a handful of his food on the box and let him eat it there. Step up on the box yourself and stamp on it so he can hear what it sounds like. Step on and off a few times. If the top of the box is hard and slippery, he will not feel secure about standing on it. Cover the top with a square of carpet to give his feet something to grip, especially if he is shod. Or, place a small handful of sand or grit on the top.

While giving your horse a cue word such as "Up," ask your horse to put either front foot on the box. At this point it doesn't matter which foot he uses, as you are giving him the chance to use whichever foot is most comfortable for him to use first. If he refuses, you may have to pick up his foot and actually place it on the box. In this case pick up his left front leg as it will be the closest to you. Most horses will snatch their foot away and put it back on the ground. Pick up his foot again and place it back on the box, while repeating your cue word. Hold it there while praising and rewarding him. Then pick up his foot and place it back on the ground. The longer you can keep his foot on the box the better. Many gentle, well-trained horses will simply step up onto the box with both front feet. If you have one of those horses, great. You get to skip a few steps!

Once your student will place one foot confidently on the box, work on getting both front feet up. The moment he places both feet on the box when cued, get excited. Clap, tell him how wonderful he is, stroke him all over, and give him his food reward. Let him stand there on the box while you praise him. Should he step back and off the box, stop your praise. Don't punish him; just stop the praise. Ask him to get back up on the box, and if he does, repeat your praise, clapping, stroking, and rewarding him. Let him stand on the box while you praise him, then turn him to the side and lead him off the box. Make getting off the box your idea — not his. Lead him around for a few minutes and ask him to get on the box again. When he clearly understands the cue "Up" and steps up onto the box with both front feet, praise and reward him and put him away.

This trick will come in handy throughout your horse's life. He should cross any bridge when asked. Simply tell him "Up," which to him means step forward and up onto something. It could be a trailer, bridge, or trail obstacle, but the conditioned response should be the same. Cue him to drop his head and look at the object, then cue him to step up onto or over it.

Repeat the training daily until he can't wait to get up on the box with his front feet. Whenever my horse is loose in

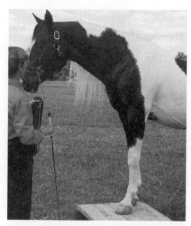

He should easily stand with both feet on the box.

the arena with the box, he runs to stand on it. Now that's a willing performer!

A word of warning: After your horse has mastered standing on a box, it is a real temptation to want to show him off to your friends. Someone who knows that your horse will stand on a box might ask you to have him put his feet up on objects such as the picnic table, the tack box, a table, or other unsuitable objects, just to see if he will do it. No one loves your horse like you do, and it's up to you to say no. Never, never allow your horse to be put into a situation in which he might get hurt. Imagine the consequences if his foot broke through the picnic table. Your horse depends on you and trusts you not to get him hurt. It's not fair to your horse (not to mention yourself) to put him at risk just to satisfy the curiosity of your friends. And worse yet, shame on you if you ruin your horse's training and trust by showing off. See everything from your horse's eyes.

Once you have mastered getting your horse's front feet on the box, the next step will be to get the back feet up. This is much more difficult for the horse to do, especially on a small box. When a horse steps forward with his right hind leg, he also wants to step forward with his diagonal left front leg. With his front feet on the box, ask him to step forward with the hind feet. As he does this, he usually will step off the box with at least one of his front feet. When he does, just let him step forward and walk off the box. Do not punish him since he did try to do as asked. You asked him to step forward and he did — right off the box — and sometimes right onto your toes! He needs to learn that he can bring his hind feet forward without also moving his front feet. This can be a very difficult movement to master, especially on a small box. By starting with a larger box that is close to the ground, you can walk him up onto it with all four feet like you were leading him onto a bridge. You can reduce the box size and increase the box height as it gets easier for him.

Put the box up against a solid wall to help him keep his body straight and to keep him from avoiding the box. A helper can come in handy at this point. Ask your horse to put both front feet up on the box. While your helper holds his head to prevent him from stepping forward off the box, you try to get his third foot up. You can lightly tap his left hind leg with a dressage-length whip while your helper gen-

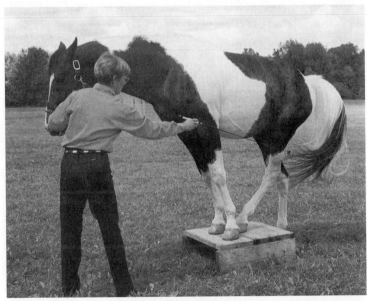

To get his back feet on the box, he must learn not to move his front feet.

Placing weight on his left hind leg enables the horse to pick up the right hind and place it on the box.

tly encourages the horse to lean forward. You might have to place his left hind foot on the box with your hands. He will probably try to pull his foot back and put it on the ground. Pick the foot up and place it back on the box again. Keep replacing the foot until he will leave it on the box — perhaps only resting his hind toe on it. Reward and praise him. Keep practicing getting three feet on the box until he's quite relaxed about it. Once he's comfortable with three feet up, push his hindquarters forward and he should step up with his fourth foot onto the box. Sometimes it takes a mighty strong push from behind since he will have to transfer his weight to the back foot on the box so he can pick up the fourth foot. When he does so, rejoice, praise, and reward him. On a larger box this is a happy moment. On a smaller box this is a monumental moment in your — and his — training!

Once your horse has mastered standing on the box with his two front feet, you can combine this trick with the

*Once all four feet are on, ask him to drop his head for
the classic "End of the Trail" pose.*

Spanish Walk (Chapter 7) cue. He will hold his position on
the box while lifting and holding up one front leg. Wait
until he can perform the Spanish Walk well, and then ask
him to put his front feet on the box. Cue him to lift one of
his front legs and keep tapping it to encourage him to hold
it up. Praise and reward him. You can also combine standing
on the box with the circus bow (Chapter 9). Your box will
need to be large enough that he will have enough room to
spread his front feet so his head will fit down between them
when he is cued to perform the circus bow.

The box stand is an excellent training exercise for even a
very young foal. Place the low box, no more than six to ten
inches high, just outside his mother's stall, where they can
still see each other. Even if the foal isn't halter broken, you
can gather him up in your arms and encourage him to get
up on the box. Place one arm around his chest and the other
around his hindquarters and push him up onto the box.
Once he's there, encourage him to relax as you give his back

A horse and rider must develop trust and teamwork to stand on a small box as the rider cannot see the box.

and itchy spots a good scratching. Praise him with your voice and then encourage him to step off. Once halter broken, he can be taught to hop up on the box himself by leading him onto it. Have him hold that position for a few minutes while you praise him and then ask him to hop down. It's an excellent exercise in teaching a colt the beginning of patience, respect, control, balance, and confidence. Teach him that he will be rewarded with praise and scratching and he will look forward to his training sessions — laying the foundation for any future training.

7

Teaching the Spanish Walk

Few things can be done under saddle that is as impressive to an audience as the Spanish Walk. It's also thrilling for the rider as he can easily feel the effort and lift the horse makes as he marches along, lifting high first one front leg, then the other. In breeds that naturally have high leg carriage, such as the Andalusian, this movement is breathtakingly beautiful, but all breeds can learn to perform a good Spanish Walk. It can be performed in hand or under saddle, but it is first taught from the ground.

What you will need: Halter, lead rope with chain, leg wraps, dressage-length whip, and treats.

What you will be doing: You will be cueing your horse to lift his front legs alternately, and to extend them in front of himself until he appears to be marching.

How to proceed: Outfit yourself in your safety helmet, gloves, and boots and your horse with his halter, lead rope, and leg wraps. Stand slightly offset to his chest and shoulder, facing toward him. Should he strike forward with a front leg, you don't want to get hit by either his knee or hoof. Begin with your horse standing still and square. Take your dressage whip and lightly tap his left front upper forearm. Most horses will usually step backward. Pull him back

The cue whip points to the cue spot for the Spanish Walk.

Tap the upper forearm until he lifts his leg.

forward and tap again. He might raise his hoof and put it back down in the same place or lift it and step back. Keep repeating the light taps. You are lightly annoying him like a biting fly would. The moment he lifts his leg and brings it forward, praise and reward him. Stroke his neck, clap, and show him how overjoyed you are with his response. Walk

As he begins to understand, ask for more extension.

him around a few minutes and let him finish chewing his treat. Stop and try it again. The first time he brought his leg forward was probably an accident so it might take a few minutes before he does it again. Ignore any other leg movement. Reward only for any forward reaching of his leg. The height of the leg is not important at this point. Once you get him to bring his leg forward a few times, reward him and put him away.

Your second training session will start the same. Tap on his left front forearm until he lifts it and brings it forward. Tap just hard enough to cause him to lift his leg.

Do not lose your temper and begin to strike him harder. Keep tapping just enough to make him want to lift his leg. If he plants his legs, tap slightly harder but not enough to sting or hurt him.

Should he ever lift his leg and stamp it down, as if in frustration, reward him profusely and take him for a little walk. This is what you are looking for.

Once you are getting him to bring his left front leg forward

Once the horse has mastered this degree of extension, teach him to lift the opposite leg.

when you give him the forearm tap, try tapping his right front forearm. He still may try to bring his left leg forward. Don't punish him; just ignore it and keep tapping his right forearm until he responds correctly.

Over the next few days to several weeks, practice each leg separately until he understands the left cue for the left leg and right cue for the right leg. Once he understands that well, start to alternate the cues and legs. He will usually do better with one leg than the other. Horses are usually stronger on one side, like people are. Don't worry about it now. Keep practicing with each leg and the legs will become more equal.

Once he is easily bringing each cued leg forward when asked, start to ask for height. Tap his forearm until he raises his leg; keep tapping until he starts to lift it higher. Reward for any up and out movement rather than just forward movement.

Lead him forward on a long lead, while you walk backward, alternately cueing each forearm. He should walk along with you well for a few steps until he's stretched out behind. He'll march on the front end until he's stretched out, and then he'll take a few steps forward with his hind feet to catch them up. Don't worry. In time he will learn to move his back feet forward as he marches forward with his front feet.

TRAINING KEY

Your horse doesn't need to stamp his foot each time, but when he does it the first and maybe the only time, he seems to understand what you are asking him to do and learns faster after that.

The Spanish Walk can easily be taught to be performed under saddle. The rider's toes can tap the shoulder area lightly so that the horse will alternately lift his front legs. You can also use a whip to cue the horse, by tapping his alternate shoulders. Some riders will cue the Spanish Walk by lifting the rein on the right side as they bump the horse's right shoulder with their toe, and alternate for the other side. Other riders merely lift alternate reins as they switch their weight from side to side. The Spanish Walk is an excellent exercise to supple and stretch your horse's legs and shoulders before a class or event.

A word of warning: You should never allow your horse to strike his foot forward without first being cued. Like rearing, some horses really seem to enjoy this movement and get too enthusiastic. Stallions also seem to like to use their front feet more than mares or geldings. The moment stallions think they are going to be asked to Spanish Walk, they start striking out with their front feet. Immediately correct your horse with a sharp "No!" and give a jerk on the lead rope and run him backward. He is to be a gentleman and wait for your cues. Never stand directly in front of your horse and stand well out of his "strike zone." Getting a hoof in your stomach or on your kneecap is not fun!

Striking, with the intent to hurt you, is dangerous and should be dealt with seriously. If your horse already wants to strike at you in an effort to hurt you, you need to correct his disrespectful behavior before even attempting to teach him the Spanish Walk. Should you fear that your horse would learn to become a striker, discontinue his Spanish Walk training. If your horse already strikes at you with the intent to harm you, even occasionally, it is very important to correct this bad behavior as it is a very strong sign of disrespect and dominance. Teaching your horse that he can only perform the Spanish Walk when you ask him — and correcting him harshly if he makes any striking movements on his own — should solve any striking problems.

8

More Tricks

While the lessons learned in teaching some responses, such as giving to pressure, have great benefits in other areas of your horse's life, some tricks are more for fun. If you intend to use your horse for exhibition or entertainment, these tricks are real audience hits, especially with children. It's always good to introduce humor into your act whenever you can. It is a real thrill to perform with your trick horse before a live audience and leave the crowd both amazed and laughing.

Honk a Bicycle Horn

What you will need: Halter, lead rope, rubber squeeze-bulb bicycle horn, and treats.

What you will be doing: You will be holding a bicycle horn up to your horse's muzzle and teaching him to honk it with his teeth.

You will need to buy a small rubber squeeze-bulb bicycle horn. Look for the sturdiest one that you can find and one that will honk with little pressure. Be sure that the rubber bulb is well attached and tough enough to withstand horse teeth.

How to proceed: Just before feeding time, honk the horn to accustom your horse to the sound. If he shows no fear from

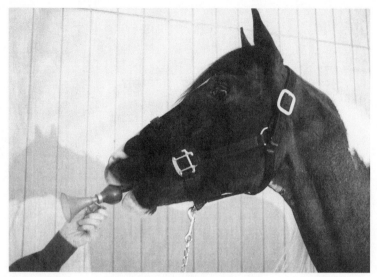

Let the horse bite the horn.

a distance, stand in front of the stall and give it a few honks. Either your horse will run to the back of his stall in alarm or the strange sound will attract him.

If he shows fear, spend more time honking the horn from time to time and dropping a handful of grain into his feed dish. Let him learn that the honking horn means something good to eat. He will soon learn to look forward to the sound.

If your horse is initially attracted to the sound, let him come up to the horn and smell it. As soon as his nose touches it, give him a reward. Give the horn a little honk and hold it up to him again. Every time he touches his nose to it, reward him. He will soon learn that when he touches the horn, he receives a reward. Once he is doing that well, honk the horn and hold it up for him. This time do not reward him for just touching it. Hopefully, he will nuzzle it and try to give it a little bite. Hold the horn in such a way that you can honk it yourself should he attempt to bite it, even if he didn't actually do it. Watch your fingers! Let him think that he made the horn honk and reward him. Soon he will be try-ing to bite and honk the rubber bulb himself.

In the beginning, praise and reward him for any good attempt to honk the horn. As he improves, reward him only for good, open-mouthed bites to the rubber bulb. Do not reward him if he just grabs the horn and tries to pull it away from you. Make sure that his bites are aimed only at the rub-ber bulb and that he acts like a gentleman at all times.

I was working in the barn once when I heard a series of horn honks. I followed the sound to the stall of a weanling miniature colt. I had been teaching him to honk the horn earlier and had left the horn on a chair in front of his stall. He had reached over his stall wall, grabbed the horn off the chair, and was madly honking it. What a ham!

Troubleshooting: If your horse will not even attempt to bite the rubber bulb, try smearing something tasty on it. Rubber doesn't taste good to most horses. Try wetting it and rubbing it in a molasses-based sweet feed, applesauce, or mashed apple. Once he finds it tastes good, he will be more willing to put it in his mouth. As soon as you can, get him to put the bulb in his mouth without the coating of goodies. He will learn that if he does, he will get a nice reward. He'll be more willing to put the nasty, non-edible thing in his mouth if a handful of edible goodies follows.

Roll a Ball

What you will need: Halter, lead rope, large beach ball or plastic barrel, and treats.

What you will be doing: You will be leading your horse up to an object, such as a plastic ball, and asking him to touch it with his nose. Once he is touching it, you will ask him to roll it.

Once you have taught your horse to reach out and honk the horn, he should easily learn to roll objects with his nose.

How to proceed: Rolling objects, especially larger ones, can initially frighten a horse. If this is the case with your horse, be patient and let him look the ball over and smell it thoroughly. If he is still frightened of it, roll the ball slowly in front of him while talking to him reassuringly. Lead him around in your training area as you bump the ball with your toes and lead him after it as it rolls. If you wish, have an assistant hold him while you slowly let it roll and bump his legs a bit to show him that it will not hurt. Act in a calm and reassuring manner and your horse should lose his fear and enjoy this trick.

Start with a large beach ball since it is easier for the horse to roll with his nose. Shop for a plastic ball that will stand up to horse bites. Lead him up to the ball. As soon as he reaches out and touches it with his nose, reward him. When he is consistently touching the ball with his nose, wait on rewarding him. He should try to touch the ball a few times, look for his reward, and then push at it. Reward him as soon as he pushes the ball. Soon you should be able to walk him up to the ball, tell him a cue word such as "Push," and he will push the ball with his nose. Reward him.

Some horses are natural pushers. They really get into the fun, and a loose ball in the pasture is good for hours of entertainment. My miniature horses like to roll the big balls by bumping them with their knees. If you have one of these naturally "pushy" horses, you can quickly teach him a cue word to push a ball on command.

As soon as he is confidently pushing the ball, you can move on to different objects such as rolling a barrel or push-

Praise and encourage the horse for his interest.

Reward him for touching the ball.

ing a baby buggy. Remember to accustom your horse thoroughly to the smell, sound, and sight of all new objects.

Crossing the Front Legs

What you will need: Halter, lead rope with chain, front leg wraps, dressage-length cue whip (optional), and treats.

What you will be doing: You will be teaching your horse

to cross his left front leg over his right. This trick looks easy but it can be difficult to master.

How to proceed: Outfit yourself with your helmet, gloves, and boots. Put a halter on your horse and take him to your training area. Stand him up square and stand by his left shoulder, facing forward. While holding his lead rope in your left hand, take his left front leg in your hands and cross it over in front of his right leg. His legs will be crossed at his ankles. Stroke his neck and encourage him to hold the pose. Most horses will pull their leg away and put it back in the original position or they will step out of the leg cross by walking to the right. If he moves, bring him back to the starting position and cross his legs again. Each time you cross his legs for him, give him a cue word such as "Cross." Pet him and try to lengthen the holding time.

The longer you can get him to hold the crossed position, the better. Reward him only when he holds the pose. A pull to the left on his halter rope will cause him to uncross his legs.

Once he is holding the crossed-leg pose well, ask him to step back out of it and try cueing him to cross his legs himself. Using your index finger or the handle of your cue whip, poke him in his left shoulder muscle at the top of his left leg and give the cue word. The pressure should make your horse step away from you to his right, since he has already learned how to move away from pressure in your earlier training sessions. If he doesn't understand, review your cues. The shoulder poke should be just hard enough to ask him to move his left front leg over, but not so long and hard as to move his entire body to the right. Have patience — this trick is harder than it seems.

At this stage the cue is a poke in the left shoulder muscle while telling him the word "Cross." Later the cue word alone should be enough for him to cross his legs, or you may choose to continue to use both the cue word and the shoulder cue at the same time. You may have to practice this movement many times until he fully understands it. This trick is very impressive when you and your horse are standing side by side, facing forward, and you both cross your legs at the same time. As you start to cross your legs, you step into his shoulder and cue him to cross his legs, by using the cue word, shoulder cue, or both. With practice this trick will become a seamless movement, and it is always a crowd pleaser.

You can also teach him an extension of this trick by cueing him to drop his head as he crosses his legs, which will give him the appearance of "playing drunk."

Troubleshooting: When you are beginning this

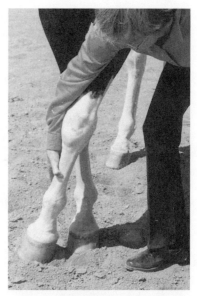

Pick up his left leg and cross it over the right.

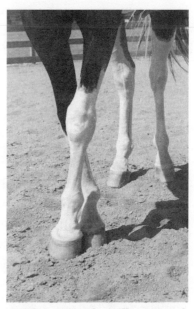

With practice he will cross and hold the position when cued.

training, it sometimes helps to stand your horse parallel to a wall on his right side. This will remove one way for him to evade this trick by discouraging him from trying to walk out of the crossed-leg position.

The Horse Laugh

What you will need: Halter, lead rope, something with a strong smell such a mentholated rub or something with an unusual feel such as a feather, and treats.

What you will be doing: You will be asking your horse to raise his upper lip to make him look like he's laughing. The horse laugh occurs when the horse lifts his upper lip in response to an unusual smell or touch (a natural reaction called the Flehman response). Stallions do this when smelling mares that are in heat. Some horses will respond with a horse laugh when they are tickled on the upper lip with a feather. Experiment where on the horse's nose you will need to tickle to get him to laugh. An unusual smell, such as a mentholated rub, held under his nostrils will often make the horse lift his upper lip. You may have to do some experimentation to find a smell that will cause the desired reaction.

How to proceed: Tickle or hold something with an unusual smell under your horse's nostrils and reward him if he lifts his lip. Use a word such as "trainer"as you cue him. Later you can work that word into a sentence such as "I am the world's best horse trainer." When your horse hears the word "trainer," he will lift his lip. Kids love this trick as it looks like the horse is laughing at you. You will find it impossible not to laugh yourself when you see your horse respond in such a funny way. It's just as funny whether done by a Shetland pony or a Clydesdale.

Troubleshooting: This is one of those tricks that a horse can't

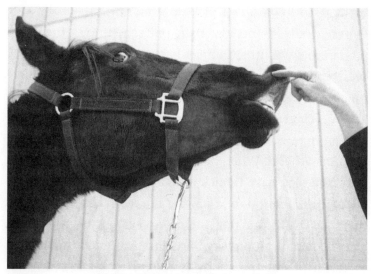

Tickle the horse under a nostril.

be forced to learn. If he doesn't want to do it, you can't make him. Some horses easily respond to a tickle or smell, and you can quickly reward them until they associate the laugh with a reward. Other horses have to be encouraged to lift their upper lip by holding a treat above their upper lips. As they lift their lip to try to reach it, reward them. You can incorporate either a cue word or a touch to their nose as the cue for the horse laugh. Others just stand there and stare at you with a dumb look. Don't give up. Have patience and experiment with different things. It's worth the extra time it may take. I have found certain horses that could master complicated tricks easily but just couldn't "get" the horse laugh. If this happens, don't worry about it. Your horse is in good company.

Picking Up Things

What you will need: Halter, lead rope, towel, and treats.

What you will be doing: You will be asking your horse first to touch and then pick up a towel. Some horses are just naturally mouthy and will pick up everything they can find. Others would sooner die than put something other than food in their mouths. Younger horses and colts are naturally more curious and usually learn this trick faster than older ones since they have the natural urge to pick up things.

How to proceed: Take your horse to his training area. Show him an item he likes such as a toy or small towel and place it on the ground. When he drops his head to sniff it, reward him. You may have to pick it up and drop it a few times to attract his attention to it. Reward him each time he touches it. When he is touching the object every time you ask or show it to him, stop rewarding him. He should reach down to touch it and then turn to look at you, expecting his reward. Wait until he touches it again and then moves it around with his nose. If he picks it up, pour on the praise, clap, and reward him well. The more you work with him, the faster he should pick it up and the longer he should hold it. Reward him each time he picks up an item. If he won't let go of the item, stick your finger in the corner of his mouth while telling him to drop it and he will release it.

Troubleshooting: If he will not pick anything up, try crushing an apple or sugar cube in a handkerchief. In trying to get to the goodie, he should pick up the cloth. He will soon associate picking up items in exchange for food rewards.

A word of warning: Remember, you may be creating a monster. Your horse could be so pleased with his new talent that everything goes into his mouth. You set a brush down and he wants to pick it up. I have a yearling filly that hasn't even started learning this trick yet. If I tie her too close to the tack rack in the barn aisle, she'll have everything knocked down or in her mouth. I have to stop what I'm doing to rescue my lead ropes and brushes. She should be one of those "natural talents" who will find this trick both fun and easy to learn.

Once your horse will pick up items for you, it can easily be worked into an act. It's great fun to drop an item and have your horse pick it up for you. He can also perform this trick while you are riding him. He can pick up an item, swing his head around, and hand it up to you. It's a real crowd pleaser. You can even work with him to open a mailbox prop, get the mail, and hand it back to you!

Remember that all tricks are based on a series of small steps. Break everything down into simple steps. Open the mailbox, pick up the mail, hand it back to you. It looks easy, but it all takes time to master. Breaking it down into steps makes it easier to train and perform.

Yes and No

What you will need: Halter, lead, a small pointed object to hold in your hand such as a blunt nail or a blunt nail file, and treats.

What you will be doing: You will be teaching your horse to shake his head for "no" and nod his head for "yes." You can usually teach the yes and no trick very easily in just a few minutes. You can use a cue word that he will associate with the physical cue that you can work into your trick act.

How to proceed: Take a small object in your hand such as a large blunt nail or a blunt nail file. Cup the object in the palm of your hand as you tap his skin. For "no," lightly tap him on the side of his neck under the area his mane covers. As you tap him with the pointed object, he should shake his head as if answering "no." Nearly every horse will respond in this way. To teach the "yes," you can lightly tap the center of his chest until he bobs his head down as if saying "yes." When he responds correctly, praise and reward him.

The cue for "no" is a tap on the side of the neck.

The cue for "yes" is a tap at the base of the neck.

These are normal responses your horse would make to a fly biting him. He tries to shake it off his neck and will try to knock it off his chest with his chin.

In your following training sessions, he should start to shake or nod his head as you bring your cue point close to his body but not touching him. Choose a cue word and repeat it as you cue him until he will respond to just the word. For example, you could choose the word "love" as your cue for "yes" or "no," depending on the response you want, and then ask him the question "Do you love me?" When he hears the cue word, and you indicate with your finger towards his cue area, he should respond accordingly. If he forgets or gets lazy, go back to using the pointed object again for a few sessions.

Troubleshooting: If your horse will not respond by either shaking his head for "no" or nodding his head for "yes," usually your cue object is too large or blunt.

Something as large and dull as your finger usually will not work in the early stages of training. As your horse learns the cue, he will learn to respond to a cue word, your finger, or a movement toward his neck or chest cue area.

A word of warning: If your horse tries to nip at you, you may be poking him too hard or your object is too sharp. Never use something like a pin as a cue object as it is way too small and sharp and can make your horse fearful or angry. You wouldn't want someone to poke you with a pin! Be careful not to use a cue word that rhymes with other common words. Examples would be "hello," "whoa," "oh no," "no," or "know," as they could easily be confusing to your horse. I've gotten some interesting responses from my horse, who knows the voice command "whoa," when I've waved to my friends and shouted, "Hello." My horse thought that I was shouting "Whoa" to him and unexpectedly slammed on the brakes.

9

Circus Bow

The circus bow occurs when the horse puts his head between his front legs and shifts his weight to the rear. In an extreme circus bow the horse's forehead will be on the ground between his front legs. This trick is an excellent exercise to stretch and supple the neck and back muscles.

What you will need: Halter, lead rope, leg wraps, and treats.

What you will be doing: You will be teaching your horse how to spread his front legs, drop his head down between his knees, and lower the front half of his body.

How to proceed: Outfit yourself with your safety helmet, gloves, and boots, and take your horse to his training area. The circus bow has several steps. The horse must first learn to spread his front legs (to fit his head between his knees) and hold that position. Then he must learn to drop his head between his legs. If he tries to put his head between his knees without naturally spreading his legs first, you will have to teach him to spread them before going on. Stand him up square. Stand by his left shoulder. Pick up his left front leg and spread his legs slightly. If he pulls his leg back to the original position, pick up his leg again and position it where you want it. Keep repeating this until he holds that position for you. With his legs spread, cue him to drop his head, and repeat your cues with a treat under his nose. If he moves his leg, takes a step back, or bows on one knee, simply stand him back up until he's standing square again.

Your patience may be tried as your horse attempts to learn this trick, especially as he learns to hold his position. Eventually, he will be able to hold that pose while he reaches down and back with his head until it is well between his front legs. Your goal is to get him to reach back even farther, until his forehead is nearly on the ground before you give him his reward.

To start the circus bow, stand your horse up square. Give him his cue to drop his head. If you've already taught your horse how to bow on one leg, as discussed in Chapter 4, he may at first think you want him to do that, and try to go down on his right front cannon bone. If he tries to bow down on his right leg, don't punish him. You worked hard to teach him the one-legged bow so don't punish him for trying to please you with it. Should he bow, simply tell him "No" and pull him forward and up onto both his front feet again. Cue him to drop his head again.

With his head down, hold a treat under his nose. A long carrot works well so you won't get your fingers nibbled as he reaches for it. When he reaches for it, pull it down and back slightly. You want him to follow the treat as you move it down and back toward his knees. Once he knows that you have a carrot for him, move your hand to between his front legs and extend the carrot or the treat far enough forward that he knows you still have it for him. He should bend his chin farther back toward his knees as he reaches for the carrot. Keep the carrot just out of his reach. As you pull your hand back between his front legs, he should put his head between his knees and reach farther and farther back for the carrot. Let him get a bite of the carrot and let him stand back up again. Don't let him take a step backward or bow on one knee. If he does, simply pull him forward into your starting position and try again.

Once he will reach down and back to follow the carrot, you're ready to ask him to reach down farther. Stand just behind his girth area on his left side. From behind his left elbow, reach under his chest and tap the bottom of his chest a few times. You are teaching him where his cue spot is. Tap the bottom of his chest and then reach with the carrot forward between his front legs and up toward his chin. Show him that you have a treat down there just waiting for him. If he steps back to try to reach it, lead him forward into his original position. Repeat your chest tap, show him the carrot, and when he reaches for it, slowly pull the carrot down and back. If he has learned to hold his front feet pose, he should reach his head down and back between his front legs. Give him his carrot and praise him.

The horse must spread his front legs wide enough to fit his head between his knees.

Instead of the tap on the bottom of the horse's chest, you could instead cue him with a tap just behind his left elbow. Once he has mastered this trick, give him his cue (whichever you have taught him); he should spread his front legs and drop his head between them. You can slowly decrease the use of your "tease" carrot until you no longer need it. A reward or praise is always welcome at the completion of the entire trick.

Once your horse has thoroughly mastered standing on a box and the circus bow, you can combine the two.

Ask your horse to stand on the box with his two front feet. Praise him. Cue him for the circus bow. He will need to spread his front feet to have enough room between his knees for his head, so make sure that the box is large enough or he might fall off the box with one or both legs. Go slowly and reassure him that what you are asking him to do is safe. Most horses that have mastered the circus bow will easily learn how to perform the same trick while their front feet are on the box. It's a real crowd pleaser.

You can also ask for the circus bow when your horse is under saddle. Raise your reins up his neck a little and jiggle them to get his attention and then tap him with the cue whip just behind his left elbow as close to his initial cue spot as possible. It might take him a moment to spread his front legs and

You can combine the circus bow with standing on a box.

then drop his head down between his knees. Remember to keep your weight well back so you aren't thrown off balance and fall too far forward. Your extra weight on his neck will make this trick more difficult for him.

10

The Buck Jump

The buck jump is a very impressive trick and is always a crowd pleaser. The horse will stand still with his front legs and kick up with both hind legs when cued. It is most commonly performed from the ground with the horse in hand. Very advanced horses can be taught to perform the buck jump under saddle, but it takes much more effort from the horse and is difficult for the rider to remain seated in the saddle. In either case the trick is taught first from the ground.

If your horse is already a bad bucker, you don't want to reinforce the habit, so you might not want to teach your horse this trick. However, most horses that have mastered all the tricks taught thus far should understand that you are teaching them a trick and they're only to do it when cued to do so. In addition, if your horse has any type of permanent back injury or muscle soreness, you also might want to skip this trick. You also should skip this trick if your horse is either very young or very old. A young horse might not have the proper bone and muscle development and an elderly, overweight, or arthritic horse might hurt himself in the effort.

What you will need: Halter, lead rope with chain, wraps for all four legs, buggy whip with no lash, and treats.

What you will be doing: You will be tapping your horse's croup with your longer cue whip just enough to encourage him to buck slightly or kick up with his hind feet.

To teach the trick, you will need a buggy-length cue whip. A whip that is too short might get you too close to the action, and a too-long whip is difficult to hang on to. Outfit your horse with good leg protection as he could easily accidentally kick himself, especially if he is wearing shoes.

How to proceed: Outfit yourself in your safety helmet, gloves, and boots. Stand beside your horse's left shoulder, facing toward his tail, and reach back with your cue whip and lightly tap the top of his croup just in front of his tail head. At first he will be confused and want to step forward or sideways. Your left hand will be holding his head steady and in position so he can't step forward. Keep up your light taps in a steady rhythm. He can't go forward since you are holding him still, yet you are tapping him to go forward. The only place he has to go is up. He should start to tuck his haunches up under himself and arch his back, like a coiled spring. He will become annoyed and should give you a little "hop up" with his hindquarters.

Immediately stop your taps, drop your whip down to your side, and

Tap lightly with the cue whip just above the tail.

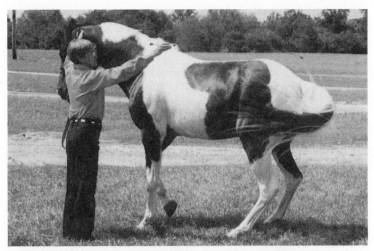

The horse should begin to tuck his hindquarters.

Praise and reward any effort to kick up behind.

greatly praise him. Walk him forward to relax him and cue him to do another trick that he enjoys and can perform easily and put him away. This will end your training session.

When you start your training session the next day, review all or a few of his tricks, then ask for the buck jump again. If he bucks up a little for you, praise him, take him for a little walk, cue for a simple trick again, and then put him away.

As the horse becomes more advanced, he will kick higher.

As your sessions continue, you should be able to ask for the buck jump and get a nice little bounce or kick up of his hind feet as he begins to understand what you are asking. This trick is easy for some horses and difficult for others. My own horse leaps and bucks in the pasture with glee, but this trick is his least favorite.

Troubleshooting: If he hurts himself by accidentally kicking or knocking his legs together as he buck jumps, he will not want to perform this trick. Be sure that his legs are well protected.

A word of warning: Needless to say, you do not want anyone standing behind him when he performs his buck jump! A horse has amazing power and reach with his hind feet. There was a real reason that warhorses were taught to kick out behind in a crowded battlefield.

It is also very important your horse understands that the buck jump is a cued trick. It's your job to make sure you cue him the exact same way each time. You do not want him "guessing" if you cued him and have him perform the buck jump in the middle of your halter class when you use your whip to knock a fly off his rump. Some horses will hop up off the ground a little with their front feet before they kick up their hind feet in the effort to perform the buck jump. It's your job to keep your feet out from under him.

This trick also can be done from the saddle when your horse becomes more advanced, but it is very difficult for the rider to stay in the saddle. When he kicks out, the power he generates will launch you forward at a surprising speed. Also, it's much harder for your horse to perform this trick with a rider's weight on his back. Thus, the buck jump under saddle is best left to professional performers and their horses.

11

The Sit

Many times when you see a trick horse sitting, he got there from lying down, not from a standing position. Sitting up is much easier for your horse to perform. It is much more difficult to train a horse to sit down flat on the ground from a standing position. However, nearly all horses will sit down when given something to sit on that is at hock height and is both soft and strong enough to support their weight. For some reason mules seem to be able to do it more easily.

A horse's back is not as flexible as a dog's, and a horse has a great fear of putting himself at risk. When a horse sits, he is basically allowing his hindquarters to "drop off into space." He can't see right behind his tail. He wants to know what's behind him and wants to be sure that what he's sitting on won't allow him to fall. Once he starts to sit, he's pretty much committed. Horses are smart critters, and you can't trick them into doing something they think will harm them. Don't lie to your horse; it will cause him to lose trust in you.

Sit Up from Lying Down

What you will need: Halter, lead rope with chain, leg wraps, and treats.

What you will be doing: You will be asking your horse to lie down and then rise into a sitting position.

How to proceed: Outfit yourself in your safety helmet, gloves, and boots. Cue your horse to lie down (Chapter 5). When he is quietly lying on his chest, lift his halter lead slightly. He should bring his legs out in front of himself as if getting ready to get up. As soon as his legs unfold and come forward, stop him. Tell him "Whoa" and pull down on his halter. Sometimes he'll lie back down, sometimes he'll leap up, and sometimes he'll stop where he is asked. Praise him only for stopping with his legs out in front. He's in an awkward position, and he usually can't hold it very long without lurching to his feet.

Cue him to lie down again. Your goal is to get him to rise to a sitting position but to stop just before he makes the effort to get up. Lift his halter and try to get him to inch up more and more without getting fully to his feet. If he holds a nice sitting position, pour on the praise. Reward him while he is sitting, so he will know the reward is for sitting and not for getting up. When you are ready for him to get up, pull up on his halter and tell him, "Get up." The goal is to teach him to wait for your cue. Don't punish him for leaping to his feet. He did lie down like you asked, but he hasn't quite got the second step figured out yet.

Practicing sitting once or twice in a training session

Lift the horse's head until he extends his front feet.

*Lift his head higher and encourage him to sit up gradually
without standing.*

Gradually increase the time and height the horse will sit.

is enough. Once horses understand what you are asking, they usually catch on pretty quickly and will hold the position more upright and longer.

You can make this trick even more exciting by standing on him. When your horse has learned how to sit up and hold that position, you can begin by sitting on him. Ask him to sit up, stop, and hold that position. Sit gently down on his haunches and praise him. Move off him and cue him to stand up. As you continue his training, cue him to sit up, stand on him for a moment, hop off, and cue him to stand up. Stand on his hip as he can best support your weight there. And, if he should get up before you ask him to, it's one of the last areas to leave the

> **REMEMBER THIS TIP**
>
> Reward him only when he's in the sitting position. Don't wait until he gets up to reward him or you will be rewarding him for getting up and not for sitting.

ground and you can easily hop off when you feel him start to rise. You may need to use his lead rope or a neck rope for balance and be ready to get off quickly, if necessary. For this adaptation be sure to wear non-slip shoes that won't dig into his back. Don't use grooming products on his back that

Stand on your horse once he masters sitting.

make the coat slippery or it will be practically impossible to stand on his sloping back. (Do not try to stand on a young horse or a horse too small to bear your weight.)

Advanced horses can lie down, sit up, and then stand back up while you are seated in the saddle. However, getting up with a rider on their back can be very difficult for some horses. If your horse seems to struggle to get to his feet, it is best to dismount before asking him to stand. Also, if you do use a saddle, it's your job to be sure that the stirrups are out of your horse's way both when he lies down and when he gets up.

Troubleshooting: Be sure that your horse has good footing to work on. If the ground is slippery, he will have trouble maintaining the position of his front feet. It will also be difficult for him to stand up if his hind feet can't get any traction.

A word of warning: Keep your feet out of his way. He'll sling his feet forward when he starts to get up and can mash toes that get in his way. Don't stand over the top of his head as he also might toss his head up quickly in his effort to get up.

Sit From the Stand

What you will need: Halter, lead rope with chain, leg wraps on all four legs, dressage-length cue whip, and treats.

What you will be doing: You will be asking your horse to sit down from a standing position onto a prop, such as a firm sawdust pile.

A word of warning: Never allow your horse to sit on something too hard such as a pile of stones or logs. His hocks and legs could easily be skinned up, and you will ruin his trust in you. Never allow him to sit on anything that can't support his weight. Don't allow friends to tempt you to show your horse off by asking him to sit on something you know, or even think, might not be safe.

Teach the horse to sit on a safe material such as sawdust.

How to proceed: Outfit yourself in your safety helmet, gloves, and boots. In the wintertime you can plow a nice big snow pile to practice on. In the summertime you can use your sawdust pile. Back your horse up until his hind legs touch the pile. Keep trying to back him up into it. He'll try to swing his hindquarters left and right, but keep his head straight and don't allow him to swing either way. If the pile is too soft, he'll just keep backing through it. If the pile is too hard, he might back up onto the top of it. He needs to be able to back into the pile until his hocks meet resistance and he can go no farther. Keep pushing him back until you see him relax his muscles and sag down onto the pile. It might be just a slight relaxation of his hindquarters, and you'll notice that he seems to be sitting a little on his hocks. Praise him with everything you have — voice, body language, and treats!

Reward him only when he is actually in the act of sitting. Don't wait until he gets up again to reward him. Keep your

REMEMBER THIS TIP

Most horses will sit when allowed to sit down on something soft yet firm enough to definitely support them at hock height. However, few horses will learn to sit down flat on the ground from a standing position.

treats in your pocket so you will be able to reach them quickly when needed. This is a big accomplishment in his trick training. He has trusted you enough to take the chance that what you were asking was safe to do. In the beginning, reward him for any sitting effort, even if it was just a slight bend at his hocks, then put him away to think about it.

Some horses will willingly relax and sag their hindquarters down onto the pile, and others will resist your best efforts. If your horse won't even try to sit, adjust the height, firmness, or softness of the sawdust pile, or change the material you are trying to get him to sit on. If he doesn't feel that the "seat" is safe, he won't sit. If he doesn't understand what you

Gradually reduce the height of the sawdust pile.

are asking him to do, he will make a few "guesses" and will try a few other things first. Keep at it, keep his head straight, and give him no other place to go but back into the pile.

As you continue your training sessions with sitting, keep asking for just a little more sit. The higher your pile, the easier it is for him to start. As he advances and feels more comfortable about sitting,

Always provide some cushion on which the horse sits.

gradually reduce the height of the pile.

Once you get your horse trying to sit pretty well when you back him up to the pile, you can begin cueing him by lightly tapping his hocks with a dressage whip.

Back him up to the pile, push him back into it, lift up on his halter, and tap his hocks all at the same time. You also can add a voice cue, "Sit," if you like.

As he advances, you should be able to back him to the pile, lift his halter, tap his hocks, and he'll sit.

Many owners have built padded chairs for their horses. On close inspection you will note that the chairs are usually at hock height, are exceptionally heavy duty and very padded, and have "anchors" that weight the chair to the ground so it doesn't move out from under the horse as he sits down. As impressive as that seems, it's actually easier for a horse to sit in a specially designed chair like this than to sit flat on the ground, from standing. As your horse advances, you can keep reducing the pile until he's on the ground. I had a little

Arab once that was so good at sitting that he did it all the time by himself. Since him I have had only a few horses that easily went from standing to sitting flat on the ground. The horse in the photos was doing it as a yearling.

Troubleshooting: If your horse won't step back farther into the pile, push on his shoulder or chest. If you use a sawdust pile, it works better if the pile is in the corner of an indoor arena. The two walls will make the pile firmer and not allow it to fall apart so easily. Using bales of hay usually doesn't work well. The horse's legs could get caught in the baling twine, and the bales tend to come apart. If the horse feels the bales won't support him, he will resist sitting on them. If you have nothing other than hay bales to use, pile them in the corner of an arena so the two walls will help keep the bales from moving. Replace any bales that break, as loose hay will not offer the support the horse needs to sit safely. The soft hay will allow him to sit down farther than he's ready to and might scare him. When he is more advanced, he might be willing to sit on hay. This is one of those tricks that seem to go well the first day, but the horse resists the second day. Don't worry. Keep at it and he will sit.

A word of warning: Don't stand directly in front of him or he might run over you if he should bolt forward. Again, keep your toes and your head out of his way. The act of pushing up against something and sitting down will "scruff" up your horse's tail. You might want to wrap it or put it in a tail bag to protect it.

If your horse's tail is very long, be sure that he doesn't stand on it and pull some hairs out, which will definitely hurt!

12

The Rear

The rear is one of those tricks that everyone wants to teach right away. It's impressive and usually pretty easy to teach, so why don't we teach that trick first?

I've been asked many times to tell someone the secrets of teaching the rear so they can teach their horse just that one trick. They're usually not interested in learning anything else and just want to be able to haul back on the reins, have their horses rear, and impress their friends with a big rear. I always tell them no, and you should, too.

There are many reasons to wait on teaching the rear. If you've been following this book, you know that you start with the simple idea of teaching your horse to give to pressure. Once he understands that, you slowly build up his muscles and, more importantly, his brain to understand more complex moves. You show your horse what you want, teach him to do it, and he understands that you are teaching him something. If you give him the same cue every time, he learns what that means and will perform for you in a willing and happy manner.

If you jerk on the reins until your horse rears, he will learn to rear. But, he will not have learned the basic steps in getting to that rear. He usually is reacting to pain the first few times and quickly figures out that to avoid the pain, he must rear. In addition to avoiding pain, he learns that you will stop when he rears.

So what can happen when a novice horseman teaches his horse only to rear? Whenever the rider jerks the reins, the horse rears. They go on a trail ride and the rider wants to show off his horse and makes the horse rear. The rider is happy and the horse is happy because he has figured out what it takes to make the rider quit jerking his mouth. Now our happy team comes to a river. The horse refuses to step into the water. The rider loses his temper after a few minutes and starts to jerk the horse around. The horse doesn't want to cross the river but knows what will make the rider stop jerking him around and also what seems to make the rider happy, so he rears. If the horse doesn't want to load into a trailer, he rears. If he doesn't want to back up in the show ring, he rears. You gave him the accidental cue and he responded by doing something he thought would please you — and make you quit jerking on him.

The rear is the one trick that can come back to haunt you if not taught correctly and in the proper order. Many horses can rear easily. If you've ever been to a horse auction and heard the auctioneer say a horse is "light in the front," it means the horse likes to rear. He is so light in the front that it's easy for him to rear. While this is not a good term to hear when looking for a kid's horse, an experienced trick trainer can put this natural talent to good use.

It is very important that your horse already has established a trick-training base so he understands that you are cueing him to rear. He must not perform this, or any other trick, unexpectedly on his own. He must always wait for your cue.

What you will need: Halter, long lead such as a lunge line, a buggy whip without the lash, leg wraps, and treats.

What you will be doing: You will be encouraging your horse to bring his front feet off the ground and then, as he advances, slowly increasing the height of his rear.

A word of warning: A horse can reach much farther forward with his front legs than you think. As he rears, he also will stand up much higher than you think. Never ask him to rear on a short lead rope or bridle reins. The lead will be quickly pulled from your hand and will leave you too close to his front hooves. Make sure there are no overhanging projections like beams, lofts, wires, and light fixtures for him to hit with his head. Outdoors is the best place to teach the rear.

How to proceed: Take your horse to his training area. Be sure to wrap his legs, as it will be easy for him to accidentally strike himself, especially if he is wearing shoes. Wear your gloves as the rope can be yanked from your hand as he goes up. Be sure to wear your riding helmet and leather boots for added safety. For this training you should use a longer lead rope. A lunge line and buggy-length cue whip, with no long lash, works well for this. Your horse must have enough lead length to rear up without pulling on his halter and without pulling your arm out of the socket.

Stand facing your horse slightly offset to the right of his left shoulder. With your cue whip, tap your horse lightly on the side of his neck very close to where the throat latch on his halter goes around the back of his cheek or jaw. If you are right-handed, hold the cue whip in your right hand. You can use your voice to encourage him by saying the word "Up" each time you tap him. Tap him on his left throat-latch area. He may toss his head up a little. When he tosses his head, stop and praise him. Repeat the tapping until he tosses his head again. Praise and reward him; then take him for a little walk. Stop him and repeat the tapping again until you get the desired head toss response. Again, praise and reward him; then put him away.

As you work on this trick each day, begin by asking your horse to perform a trick that is easy for him. Reward him and show him that you are very happy with him. He still doesn't understand that you want him to rear up yet, but he knows that you are trying to teach him something. You can almost see the wheels turning in his head as he's trying to figure it out. This is the beauty of trick training. You aren't using pain to train him, but you are encouraging him to use his brain to figure it out. As mentioned in Chapter 1, once you have trick-trained a few horses, it will be much easier for you. Your

Reward any effort the horse makes to lift his front feet off the ground when cued.

first horse will take longer as you won't be as good yet at explaining to your horse what you want him to do.

In your subsequent training sessions gradually ask for more head toss. If he just stands there ignoring

you, tap a little harder. Try tapping him a little farther back on his neck. What you are looking for is the day his front feet hop up off the ground slightly. He might do this right away or it might take a few days. As soon as you do get a little hop, praise him with all you've got. Use your voice to tell

The horse must understand that the rear is performed only when asked. This requires a solid training foundation.

him how good he is, give him a food reward, and take him for a little walk. This is what you want him to do, so be sure to show him how happy it makes you.

In your following sessions ask for more of a hop until you are getting him to go higher each time. Praise him for each tiny hop, but give a food reward only for a response that looks like a small rear to you. Be careful, as he can strike out with his front feet as he goes up. The lunge line and buggy-length whip should keep you far enough away from his legs and out of harm's way. He can also strike out and get his front legs over the lead rope. If this happens, let him come down and calmly untangle his legs.

Horses all seem to rear a little differently. Some rear and strike out with one or both front feet while others rear and neatly fold their knees under themselves. Let your horse develop his own style and let him do what is most comfortable for him. As he advances, he may change his rearing style and be able to hold it longer.

As he begins to understand the rear cue, start lifting your whip above your head, with your arm outstretched, and give him the voice command "Up."

When your horse has mastered this trick, the cue for the rear will be the whip held straight up over your head and a voice cue of "Up," or whatever word you have chosen.

After he has mastered rearing, you can work on keeping him standing longer on his hind legs. Some horses have natural balance, and it's easy for them to stay up longer. Others just want to pop up and come right down. You can help your horse stay up longer by holding your whip up and circling it in the air above your head. Lightly tapping his front legs can also encourage him to stay up longer.

You can build on this trick and have your horse rear under

saddle. The cue is the whip being brought up alongside his right shoulder and then held up over your head while you squeeze him forward with your legs. Your rein hand will jiggle the bit in his mouth at the same time to encourage him to lighten up his front end. The bit tells him to hold his position and lighten up while your legs tell him to compress his body forward. When you give him the whip cue, he will be ready to lift up into lightly a pretty rear. You can't ask him to rear if you have not prepared him to be ready for your cue. If he's sleeping or all sprawled out, he won't be coiled and ready to respond to your cues, and the results won't be pretty.

A word of warning: This is a trick that requires that you never take your attention off your horse. You are standing in the direct line of some awesome artillery — his front legs. As in the buck jump, your job is to stay out of his strike zone. It's also your job to keep others back as well. A horse that rears too high can lose his balance and flip over backward. This can injure the horse and seriously flatten a rider. When a horse rears with a rider aboard, the horse's balance is affected, making the rear more difficult. When a horse rears, it's important for the rider to lean forward slightly. If the rider jerks on the reins or leans backward, he can pull a horse right over backward on himself.

If you feel that your horse rears too high, be sure that your cues aren't too strong. Don't reward him for any rear that is too high. You can help a horse regain his balance in a rear that is too high by quickly leaning all your weight forward onto his neck. Never hold on by pulling on the reins. Never ask your horse to rear on a slippery surface like a city street. While a rear in front of a crowd at a parade would be impressive, a fall on the slippery street would not be much of an ego booster and could result in injury to yourself and your horse.

You also must be careful with your cues so that you're not accidentally sending him signals to rear. An example might be if you suddenly brought your right cue arm and whip up over your head to wave to someone. He may glance out of the corner of his eye and see your arm giving him the rear cue. His rear response might catch you off guard. This is one of the main reasons to carry a cue whip only when you are training or performing tricks.

Conclusion

Trick training has given my horses and me many rewards. We have been invited to perform all across the country. My horses have been featured in magazines and on television. In addition to the thrill of owning and handling a trick horse, there are many more benefits. It is impossible not to develop a deeper bond with your horse after all the close contact and extra training hours you will spend with him.

Among the many benefits of having a trick-trained horse is having a horse that is more flexible, submissive, and responsive, as well as more attuned to your voice, body language, and aids. These behaviors will help your horse throughout his entire life. Whether you show, trail ride, do search and rescue, camp, ride in parades, or just have a horse in your backyard for the kids to enjoy, you can improve your horse in many ways with trick training.

Trick training is not something that can be rushed and mastered overnight. You cannot use force and cruelty and have a happy trick horse. You cannot start at the top and bask in the glory of owning a performance horse without first starting at the beginning. There will be ups and downs — days that you think your horse will never understand what you want him to do. You need to stick to it. Find out what works and what doesn't. What works for one horse might not work for another.

I have found that there is something about working with horses that benefits people as well. Many others also are discovering that working closely with horses can lift the human soul. Some therapists are using horses to work with troubled teens and adults. Often, these are people who have had no prior experience with horses. Rather than having a group session in a therapist's office, where they can only talk, some are now lucky enough to be working with horses. By being given an assignment they are to accomplish with the horse, such as teaching it to be led without a halter, they learn many skills. First they must think about the task at hand, break it down into steps, explain what they plan to do and why they think it will work, and then try to do it. They find that everything isn't as easy as they think it would be. They will have to practice, have patience, and learn teamwork. And, if it doesn't work the first time, they will have to determine why it didn't work, improve their methods, try again, and stick to it. When they do have success, they can be proud of their accomplishments, which is something that some kids never get to feel. It's a new way to learn things that they might not have otherwise.

Trick training is another way to enjoy your relationship with your horse. With the correct training, he will become a better horse for it. You will enjoy him more, take greater pride in him, and perhaps provide that extra care to make him as healthy and happy in both his body and his mind as he can be.

What do the horses think about trick training? I keep a few broodmares, and each spring they have new foals. There is an automatic water bowl in their pasture. The older horses know how to push the paddle down with their nose to get the water to run into the bowl, so they can drink. The paddle pushes down hard and the water gushes in with a lot of sputtering and splashing that the older horses ignore. It is frightening to the foals, however. They stand back bug-eyed and watch the older horses drink.

When the foals stood staring at the bowl wanting water but unable to make it work, we used to run out and push the paddle down for them. Once the bowl was filled, they would drink it empty, and we'd repeat the process until they were done. One day we looked out to see a mare drinking and her foal sadly watching her, knowing that he couldn't do it himself. We watched as the mare drank her fill. Then, to our amazement, she pushed the paddle down until the bowl filled. Without drinking the water, she stepped back and let the foal drink it empty. She refilled the bowl for him and stepped back again until he drank it empty again. In the following years, all the mares have done this for their new foals each year. Did they learn it from watching us? Did one smart mare figure it out and teach the other mares? We don't know, but it sure is something to wonder about!

Good luck with your training!

Appendix:
Tying a Running Loop

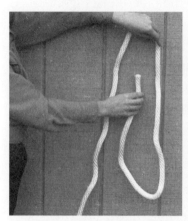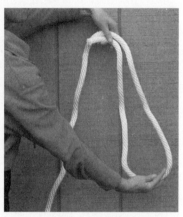

1) Start with a soft, non-stretchy, half-inch round, braided nylon or cotton rope. Use a 15-foot rope for an average-sized horse. 2) Fold back 20 inches from one end of rope.

3) Grasping the folded end cross the loop over the rope near your left hand. 4) Reach through the new loop you created and grasp the folded end of the first loop and pull it through.

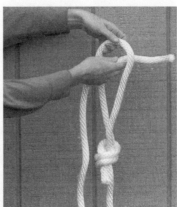

5) You now have a 4-5 inch non-slip loop in one end of your rope. 6) Run the other end of the rope through your newly created loop.

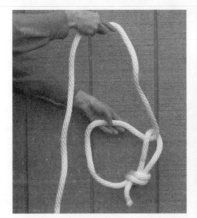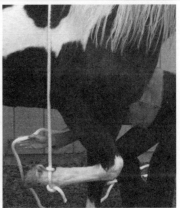

7) You now have a running loop. 8) Loop the running loop around your horse's right front ankle, just above the hoof.

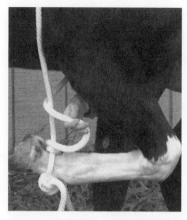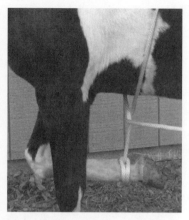

9) Run the leg rope from the right ankle up and over the horse's back. Standing on the horse's left side, lift the leg rope until the horse's cannon bone is parallel to the ground. To make holding the rope easier, you can wrap the rope once around the leg rope under the belly so the weight of the leg is held up by the horse's back. Do not tie the leg up. 10) A close-up view of how the rope can be wrapped once around the leg rope. You then hold the free end of the rope to keep the leg up.

11) Hold the leg rope in your right hand. To keep the leg lifted, use your left hand on the lead rope to cue your horse to drop his head and to shift his weight to the rear. As he relaxes he will drop down onto his right front cannon bone. Praise and reward him and release the leg rope. Once you let go of the leg rope he is free to stand back up on all four feet again.

How to Build a Training Platform:

What you Need

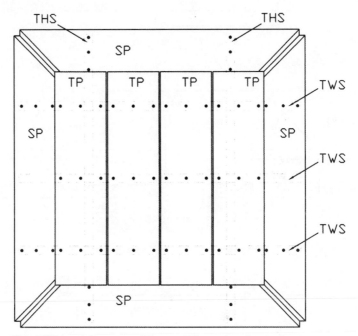

– Top View – (Plywood not shown)

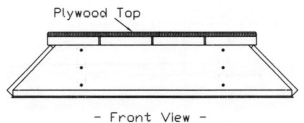

– Front View –

Material List

3 pcs. 2"x10"x12' Yellow Pine
2 pcs. 2"x12"x12' Yellow Pine
1 pc. 3/4"x37 3/4" square Plywood
60 pcs. # 8 x 3" Coarse Drywall Screws
28 pcs. # 6 x 2" Coarse Drywall Screws
1 Bottle – Wood Glue

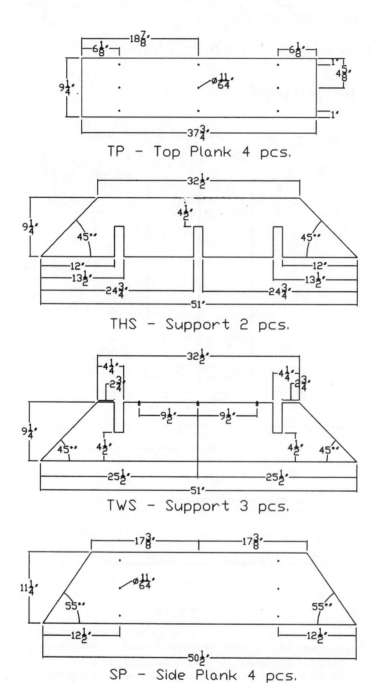

TP – Top Plank 4 pcs.

THS – Support 2 pcs.

TWS – Support 3 pcs.

SP – Side Plank 4 pcs.

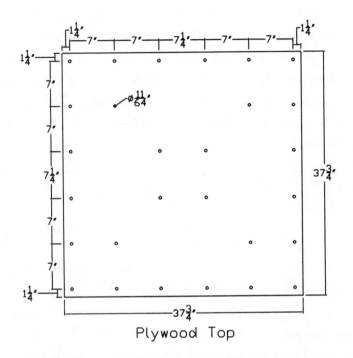

Plywood Top

Assembly Instructions for Training Platform

1) Safety first — wear approved safety equipment for the power tools you are using while working on this project.

2) Using the 2"x12"x12' material cut 4 pieces 50½" long. These make the SP (side plank) boards.

3) Using one of the 2"x10"x12' cut 2 pieces 51" long and 1 piece 37¾" long. These will make the 2 THS supports and 1 of the TP (top planks).

4) Using one of the 2"x12"x12' cut 2 pieces 51" long and 1 piece 37¾" long. These will make 2 of the TWS supports and 1 of the top planks.

5) Using one of the 2"x12"x12' cut 1 piece 51" long and 2 pieces 37¾" long. These will make 1 of the TWS supports and 2 of the top planks.

6) Cut plywood material to 37¾" x 37¾". Drill the holes.

7) Drill the holes in the TP pieces.

8) Cut the angled ends and notches on the THS pieces.

9) On the top edge of the TWS pieces make 3 pencil marks.

10) One mark is on the centerline and there is a mark 9½" on either side of it. These will be used when assembly begins to get the planks centered and make the assembly square. Cut the angled ends and notches.

11) Drill holes, cut the angled ends on SP pieces.

12) Place the 3 TWS pieces on a smooth surface with the notches facing up. Spread glue in the notches.

13) Place the 2 THS pieces into the TWS pieces. Spread glue on top of all TWS and THS pieces.

14) Place the TP pieces on the assembly and line up using the pencil marks on the TWS pieces. Measuring from the edge of the TWS to the ends of the TP, center the planks. There should be ¼" space between the TP pieces. Temporarily set the plywood top to check for squareness and fit of all pieces.

15) Remove the plywood top and then using the #8 x 3" drywall screws fasten the TP pieces to the TWS pieces.

16) Spread glue on the THS and TWS pieces where the SP pieces attach. Using the #8 x 3" drywall screws attach the SP pieces.

17) Spread glue on the THS and TWS pieces where the SP pieces attach. Using the #6 x 2" drywall screws attach the SP pieces.

18) Using a router or sander, round the edges on the plywood top so they no longer have a sharp edge.

19) It is best to store your finished training platform indoors. I have found that a two–wheel dolly makes it easy to move even over slightly rough terrain.

20) Fit and nail down a piece of carpeting or rubber matting to the top of the box to improve traction and reduce noise.

About the Author

Jan Sharp has trained show, sport, and exhibition trick horses for nearly 40 years. She has earned 24 world and reserve championships. Her stallion TS Black Tie Affair is a World Show All-Around Pleasure High Point Champion. Sharp has written for numerous publications and gives demonstrations around the country.

Sharp, who owns ten half-Arabian, black-and-white Pinto horses, lives in Ashtabula, Ohio.

Jeff Kirkbride Photography

Photo credits: outdoor photos by Lori Spellman, indoor photos by Leary Productions. Back cover photo by Jeff Kirkbride Photography.

The Horse Health Care Library

The Horse Health Care Library:

- Understanding Basic Horse Care
- Understanding Breeding Management
- Understanding the Broodmare
- Understanding EPM
- Understanding Equine Acupuncture
- Understanding Equine Business Basics
- Understanding Equine Colic
- Understanding Equine First Aid
- Understanding the Equine Foot
- Understanding Equine Lameness
- Understanding Equine Law
- Understanding Equine Medications
- Understanding Equine Neurological Disorders
- Understanding Equine Nutrition
- Understanding Equine Preventive Medicine
- Understanding the Foal
- Understanding Horse Behavior
- Understanding Laminitis
- Understanding the Older Horse
- Understanding the Pony
- Understanding the Stallion
- Understanding the Young Horse
- The New Equine Sports Therapy
- Horse Theft Prevention Handbook

Videos from The Blood-Horse New Video Collection:

- Conformation: How to Buy a Winner
- First Aid for Horses
- Lameness in the Horse
- Owning Thoroughbreds
- Sales Preparation
- Insider's Guide to Buying at Auction
- The Expert's Guide to Buying Weanlings

Call Toll-Free: **1.800.582.5604**
or order online at: **www.ExclusivelyEquine.com**

ECLIPSE PRESS

A DIVISION OF BLOOD-HORSE PUBLICATIONS / Publishers since 1916